T H E   B O O K   O F

THAI COOKING

THE BOOK OF

THAI COOKING

HILAIRE WALDEN

Photographed by
DAVID GILL

HPBooks
a division of
PRICE STERN SLOAN

ANOTHER BEST SELLING VOLUME FROM HPBOOKS

HPBooks
A division of Price Stern Sloan, Inc.
11150 Olympic Boulevard
Suite 650
Los Angeles, California 90064
9 8 7 6 5 4 3 2 1

By arrangement with Salamander Books Ltd.

This book was created by Patrick McLeavey & Partners,
21-22 Great Sutton Street, London EC1V 0DN

Art Director: Sue Storey
Editor: Barbara Croxford
Photographer: David Gill
Home Economist: Meg Jansz
Typeset by: Maron Graphics Ltd, Wembley
Colour separation by: Scantrans Pte. Ltd, Singapore
Printed in Belgium by Proost International Book Production

CONTENTS

INTRODUCTION

Thai food is an original and rich amalgam of evocative aromas, subtle blends of herbs and spices and contrasting textures and tastes. It contains flavors and techniques that are familiar from Chinese, Indian and Japanese cooking, but they have been so skillfully combined and refined that the resulting dishes have a new and exciting character.

The dishes are light and fresh. Vegetables are important, and are quickly cooked to retain their crispness, flavor and nutrients. Dairy products are not used and fish and poultry feature more prominently than meat; and where this is used it often only constitutes a small portion of the dish.

Equipment is minimal and simple, and the basic preparation of the food and its cooking is straightforward. Thai dishes are cooked quickly, with many taking only a few minutes, and the majority no more than 8 to 12 minutes. This factor, coupled with the informal way in which the dishes can be served and eaten, everyone helping themselves, make a Thai meal ideal for today's style of casual entertaining.

Although traditionally all the dishes are served at once, Thai food is so adaptable that there is no problem in dividing it into Western-style courses. Many of the dishes can also be served as snacks or simple one-dish meals.

THE TASTE OF THAI

The flavors that characterize Thai food are the citrus-limes, spiked with clean pine notes, fresh cilantro, coconut milk, garlic and chiles. A fresh sweet-sour taste is also typically Thai, derived from tangy lime or tamarind and palm sugar. Mild fish sauce provides the main savory flavoring.

Rice is a very important part of the diet. As well as being the foundation of many one course dishes, rice plays a vital supporting role for other dishes, and dilutes highly spiced ones. A point worth remembering when eating Thai food is that dishes are created specifically to be mixed and eaten with rice.

Thai curries are a case in point, as they can be searingly hot. Unlike Indian curries, Thai curries are cooked quickly and do not have the rich heaviness that results from long, slow simmering. Coconut milk is used to soften the pungency of the spices and combines flavors to give a sophisticated subtlety to the finished dish.

Thailand has a long coastline and many inland rivers, which provide fish and shellfish which are both ubiquitous and varied. Freshwater and ocean fish are frequently cooked whole with the head and tail intact, having been cleaned beforehand.

Meat is considered more of a luxury and is often 'stretched' by combining with vegetables, rice, noodles, fish or shellfish or plenty of coconut based sauce. Chicken is more abundant, but the birds are smaller than Western farm reared ones. Duck is popular, particularly for special occasions. Many vegetables are used but they are not often cooked on their own or served as a specific dish. Instead they are combined with meat, poultry or fish, and eaten as a salad, either hot or cold, or simply served with 'Nam Prik' (see page 23). The appearance of food matters to the Thais, and they like to add beautifully sculptured garnishes of fruit or vegetables to the finished dishes.

EATING THAI FOOD

Thais eat about 3 cups of rice a day. They might start with a rice soup, perhaps spooned over an egg, or simple fried rice. Lunch will be a composite rice or noodle soup, followed by crisp-fried noodles tossed with a little fish or meat, vegetables or flavorings.

The main meal is eaten in the evening, preferably in the company of an extended family and several friends. Traditionally, Thais will eat sitting on plump cushions set around a low table. All dishes are served simultaneously, rather than as separate courses, and everyone shares them.

Surrounding the large central bowl of rice there will be several dishes giving a balanced selection of flavors and textures. Usually they will consist of a soft steamed dish contrasted by a crisp fried one; one that is strongly flavored (usually 'fired' by chiles), matched by a bland one. There are

cool, crunchy salads, bowls of sauces, plus a small bowl of clear soup for each diner.

There is no structure to the meal. Every diner dips into any dish they choose, putting a portion on their plate to mix with rice. The helpings are always small, but several helpings may be taken from each dish. An ordinary family meal ends with an array of fresh tropical fruits: mangosteens, rambutans, mangoes, papayas and lychees; all neatly sliced and arranged for everyone to share. Desserts only appear on special occasions or at formal banquets.

Thais like to eat little and often so throughout the day they will buy ready made sweets, cakes and savory snacks from the numerous street vendors. Some of these savory snacks such as Pork & Noodle Balls (page 39) and Stuffed Eggs (page 35) could be served as a Western-style first course.

—COOKING AND EQUIPMENT—

The majority of Thai cooking is done in one piece of cooking equipment, the wok, by either of two very straightforward cooking methods, steaming or stir-frying. Stir-frying is a very rapid process as the ingredients are cut into small, even pieces. For successful stir-frying, heat the wok before adding the oil to help prevent food from sticking, then heat the oil until it is almost smoking before adding the ingredients. Toss the food during cooking, and keep it moving from the center of the wok to the sides. Because of its curved shape, the wok allows the food to be quickly tossed without spilling. As the food is kept moving during stir-frying, very little oil is needed.

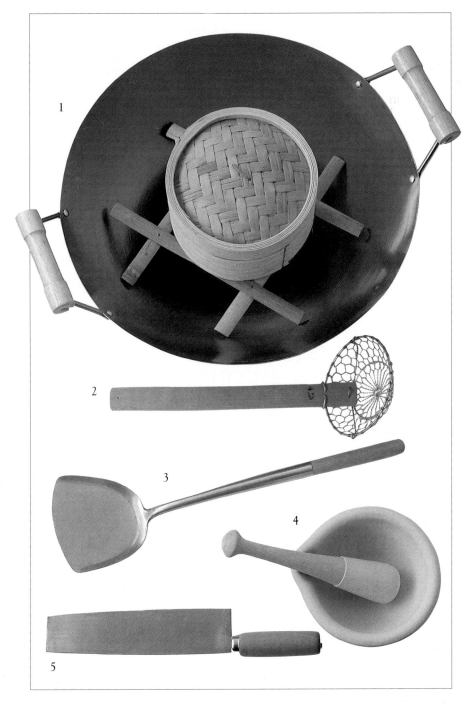

1 wok with small bamboo steamer and rack; 2 bamboo handled wire basket; 3 spatula; 4 pestle and mortar; 5 cleaver.

Equipment

The amount of equipment needed for Thai cooking is minimal. Moreover, it is possible to prepare and cook Thai food using equipment that is readily at hand in most Western kitchens, but even authentic equipment is now familiar and readily available due to the popularity of Chinese cooking.

Wok—used for frying, stir-frying, deep-frying and steaming. A useful size to buy is about 12 to 14 inches in diameter across the top. Choose one that has good deep sides and some weight. Carbon steel is preferable to light stainless steel or aluminum as these tend to develop hot spots which cause sticking, and do not withstand intense heat so well. Non-stick woks and electric ones do not reach sufficiently high temperatures.

A skillet could be used for frying and stir-frying, a deep-fat fryer for deep frying and a saucepan for steaming.

Wok stand—metal ring or stand to hold wok steady over the heat.

Rack—for using in a wok when steaming to support the steaming basket or container of food above the level of the water.

Steamer—Chinese-style bamboo steamers are used in Thailand, but Western metal ones will do just as well.

Rice cooker—because of the amount of rice Thais eat and the number of people cooked for, many households now use an electric rice cooker. A heavy saucepan with a tight-fitting cover will be adequate for Western needs.

Pestle and mortar—Used during the preparation of the majority of savory dishes. A small food processor or a coffee grinder kept specifically for the purpose will take away the effort but will not produce quite the same results. When used for fibrous ingredients such as galangal and lemon grass, the pestle and mortar crushes the fibers rather than cuts them and so releases the flavoring juices and oils more successfully.

Knives—Thais use cleavers, but a selection of sizes of good quality sharp knives will suffice.

Spatula—a long handled spatula that is curved and shaped like a shovel for scooping and tossing food in the wok.

Wire baskets—Almost without exception, Thai kitchens have a set of bamboo-handled wire baskets so they can quickly and easily plunge noodles into boiling water for the requisite short cooking time, and then speedily lift them out; different baskets are used for different types of noodles.

INGREDIENTS

Although some of the foods, principally vegetables, that are available in Thailand cannot be found in the West, a sufficiently wide range of ingredients can be obtained to produce authentic Thai dishes. All of the ingredients used in this book can be found without difficulty in Oriental and Indian stores, and are becoming increasingly available in good food stores and supermarkets.

Suitable alternatives have been mentioned where possible, although they may change the flavor of a recipe.

Banana leaves—used to make containers for steamed foods, to which they impart a delicate taste.

Basil leaves—Thai basil leaves, also called 'holy' basil, are darker and their flavor slightly deeper, less 'fresh' than ordinary sweet basil. Bundles of leaves can be frozen whole in a plastic bag for up to about 2 weeks; remove leaves as required and add straight to dishes. Substitute Thai sweet basil or ordinary sweet basil, if necessary.

Chiles—add flavor as well as 'hotness'. Thais favor small and very fiery 'bird's eye' chiles but elsewhere these are only available in Thai markets. Chiles are rarely labelled with the variety or an indication of 'hotness' so, as a rule of thumb, smaller varieties are invariably hotter than large ones. Dried chiles have a more earthy, fruity flavor.

The seeds and white veins inside a chile are not only hotter than the flesh, but have less flavor, and are generally removed before using. Chiles contain an oil that can make the eyes and even the skin sting, so wash your hands after preparing them and avoid touching your eyes or mouth.

To be really safe, wear rubber gloves when handling chiles.

Chinese black mushrooms—these dried mushrooms have quite a pronounced flavor and must be soaked for 20 to 30 minutes before use. The stalks tend to be tough so are usually discarded. Available in Oriental food stores.

Coconut cream—the layer that forms on the top of coconut milk.

Coconut milk—not the liquid from inside a coconut, but extracted from shredded coconut flesh that has been soaked in water. Soak the shredded flesh of 1 medium coconut in 1-1/4 cups boiling water 30 minutes. Turn into a strainer lined with muslin or cheesecloth and squeeze the cloth hard to extract as much liquid as possible. Coconut milk can also be made from unsweetened shredded coconut soaked in boiling water, or milk which will be richer. Allow 1-1/4 cups liquid to 2-2/3 cups shredded coconut. Put into a blender and mix 1 minute. Refrigerate coconut milk.

Ready-prepared coconut milk is sold canned (which affects the flavor slightly) and in plastic containers.

Cilantro leaves—best bought in large bunches rather than small packages. Stand whole bunches in cold water in refrigerator.

Cilantro roots—roots have a more muted taste than the leaves. Large cilantro bunches sold in Middle Eastern stores often include the roots. Fresh roots will last for several days if kept wrapped in the refrigerator, or can be frozen. If unavailable, use cilantro stalks.

Fish sauce (nam pla)—a clear brown liquid, rich in protein and B vitamins

1 *galangal*; 2 *gingerroot*; 3 *cilantro*; 4 *Chinese black mushrooms*; 5 *chiles*; 6 *Thai sweet basil*;
7 *Thai holy basil.*

that is the essential Thai seasoning. It is salty but the flavor is mild.

Galangal (galangale, laos, lengk haus) —there are two varieties, lesser and greater. The latter is preferred and more likely to be found in the West. It looks similar to gingerroot but the skin is thinner, paler, more transluscent and tinged with pink. Its flavor is also similar to ginger but less hot and with definite seductive citrus, pine notes. To use, peel and thinly slice or chop. The whole root will keep for up to 2 weeks if wrapped in paper and kept in the cool drawer of the refrigerator. Or it can be frozen. Allow to defrost just sufficiently to enable the amount required to be sliced off, then return the root to the freezer. Galangal is also sold dried as a powder or slices; the latter giving the better flavor. Substitute 1 dried slice or 1 teaspoon powder to each 1/2 inch used in a recipe; in recipes where fresh galangal is pounded with other spices, mix the dried form in after the pounding; elsewhere, use as normal.

Alternatively, use fresh gingerroot.

Gingerroot—When buying fresh gingerroot, choose firm, heavy pieces that have a slight sheen. To stow, wrap in paper towels, place in a plastic bag and store in the vegetable drawer of the refrigerator.

Kaffir limes—slightly smaller than ordinary limes with dark green, knobby peel. The smell and taste of the peel resemble aromatic lime with hints of lemon. The peel of ordinary limes can be substituted. These limes are difficult to find outside of Thailand.

Kaffir lime leaves—the smooth, dark green leaves give an aromatic, clean citrus-pine flavor and smell. They keep well in a cool place and can be frozen.

Use ordinary lime peel if kaffir lime leaves are unavailable, substituting 1-1/2 teaspoons finely grated peel for 1 kaffir lime leaf.

Lemon grass—a long, slim bulb with a lemon-citrus flavor. To use, cut off the root tip, peel off the tough outer layers and cut away the top part of stalk. The stalks will keep for several days in the refrigerator, or they can be chopped and frozen. If unavailable, use the grated peel of 1/2 lemon in place of 1 stalk.

Long beans—although these can grow to over 3 feet it is best to use younger, smaller ones. Green beans can replace them.

Mint—Thai mint has a spearmint flavor. If not available, Western spearmint or garden mint are the best substitutes.

Noodles—most types are interchangeable but two, rice stick noodles and mung bean noodles, can be crisp-fried. Dried noodles are usually soaked in cold water for 10 to 20 minutes until softened, before cooking; in general, the weight will have doubled after soaking. After draining, the cooking will usually be brief.

Mung bean noodles (glass, shining, bean thread or cellophane noodles)— tough and semi-transparent raw, they are soaked in warm water before cooking, when they turn to a jelly-like texture.

Fresh rice noodles—packaged cooked and wet in wide, pliable 'hanks'. To use, without unwinding, cut into ribbons and stir into a dish just to warm through.

Rice stick noodles (rice vermicelli)— thin, brittle and semi-transluscent, they are sold in bundles. For most uses the noodles must be soaked before cooking, but when they are to be served crisp they are used dry.

Egg noodles—these thin wheat flour-based noodles are sold in both fresh (which do not need soaking) and dry 'nests'.

Palm sugar—brown sugar with a slight caramelized flavor. Sold in cakes. If unavailable, substitute 1/2 white and 1/2 Demerera sugars.

Pandanus (screwpine)—both the leaves and the distilled essence of the flowers, called kewra water or essence, are used to give an exotic, musky, grassy flavor to sweet dishes.

Pea eggplant—very small eggplants about the size of a pea, and usually the same color, although they can be white, purple or yellow. The fresh, slightly bitter taste is used raw in hot sauces and cooked in curries.

Rice—Thais mainly use a good quality variety of long-grain white rice called 'fragrant' rice. Ordinary long-grain white rice can be substituted. To cook, rinse the rice several times in cold running water. Put the rice into a heavy saucepan with 1-1/4 cups water, cover and bring quickly to a boil. Uncover and stir vigorously until the water has evaporated. Reduce the heat to very low, cover the pan tightly with foil, then cover. Steam 20 minutes until the rice is tender, light, fluffy and every grain is separate.

'Sticky' or 'glutinous' rice—an aptly-named short, round grain variety. It can be formed into balls and eaten with fingers, or used for desserts.

Ground browned rice—sometimes added to dishes to give texture; for this, dry-fry uncooked long-grain white rice until well-browned, then grind finely.

Shallots—Thai red shallots are smaller than Western shallots. They have quite a pronounced flavor that is almost fruity rather than pungent. Ordinary shallots can be substituted.

Shrimp, dried—whole dried shrimp used to add texture and an attractive flavor.

Shrimp paste—a pungent, salty paste that is packed in jars, cans and plastic packets. It should be kept refrigerated.

Tamarind—sold in sticky brown-black blocks and provides a sharp, slightly fruity taste. To make tamarind water, break off a 1-ounce piece, pour over 1-1/4 cups boiling water. Break up the lump with a spoon, then leave about 30 minutes, stirring occasionally. Strain off the tamarind water, pressing on the pulp; discard the remaining debris. Keep the water in a jar in the refrigerator for up to 5 days. Ready-to-use tamarind syrup can sometimes be bought; it is usually more concentrated, so less is used.

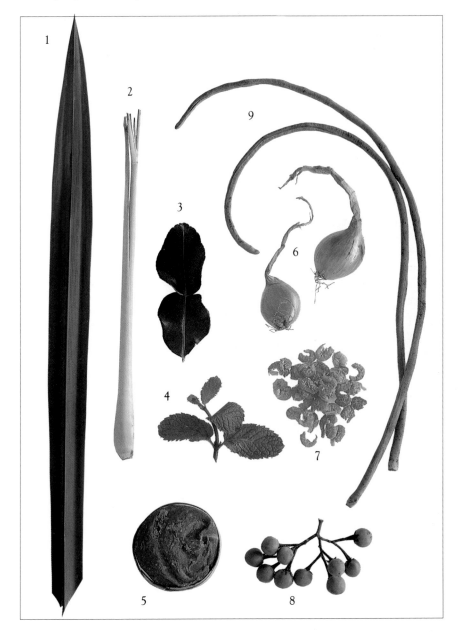

1 *pandanus leaf;* 2 *lemon grass;* 3 *kaffir lime leaves;* 4 *Thai mint;* 5 *palm sugar;* 6 *shallots;*
7 *dried shrimp;* 8 *pea eggplants;* 9 *long beans.*

──── GREEN ONION BRUSHES ────

4 green onions

Trim away some of green tops of each green onion. Cut off each white bulb where it starts to turn green.

Using a small pair of kitchen scissors, make a cut from dark green end of a leaf to about halfway along the length. Continue to cut leaf into thin strips. Repeat with remaining leaves.

Place green onion into a bowl of chilled water. Let stand a few seconds for strips to curl; check by lifting from water several times that they do not curl too tightly. Repeat with remaining green onions. Place on paper towels to dry before using.

Makes 4.

CHILE FLOWERS

4 small chiles

Cut off tip of 1 chile. Insert scissors in hole and cut through chile flesh almost to stem end. Give chile a quarter turn, make another similar cut, then repeat twice more.

Remove and discard seeds. Cut through each quarter once or twice more to make thin petals.

Place chile in a bowl of chilled water. Let stand 5 to 10 minutes for petals to open into a flower shape. Repeat with remaining chiles. Place on paper towels to dry before using.

Makes 4.

BANANA LEAF CUPS

8 pieces banana leaf, each about 5 inches square

Place two pieces of banana leaf with dull sides facing each other. Invert a bowl measuring 4 inches in diameter on top of leaves. Cut around bowl.

Form a 2-inch pleat about 1-1/2 inches deep in the edge of banana leaf circle. Staple together.

Make an identical pleat in the opposite side of the circle, then repeat twice more at points equidistant among the two pleats, to make a slightly opened, squared-off cup. Repeat with remaining pieces of banana leaf.

Makes 4 cups.

CARROT FLOWERS

1 young tender carrot, peeled

Hold carrot pointed end down. Using a small, sharp knife, make a cut toward the point to form a petal-shape. Take care not to slice all the way through. Repeat cuts around carrot to make a 4-petalled flower.

Angle knife slightly, then apply light pressure to separate carrot flower from carrot. For first few flowers, it may be necessary to ease every petal in this way, but with a little practice, flowers will come away easily with a twist of the knife.

Repeat along length of carrot. Arrange flowers individually or group them into clusters.

Note: To improve color, drop flowers in boiling water 1 minute, then drain and rinse under cold running water. Dry well.

GREEN CURRY PASTE

2 teaspoons coriander seeds
1 teaspoon cumin seeds
1 teaspoon peppercorns
8 fresh green chiles, seeded, chopped
3 shallots, chopped
4 garlic cloves, crushed
3 cilantro roots, chopped
1-inch piece galangal, chopped
2 stalks lemon grass, chopped
2 kaffir lime leaves, chopped
2 teaspoons shrimp paste
2 tablespoons chopped cilantro leaves

Heat a wok, add coriander seeds and cumin seeds and heat until aroma changes.

Using a pestle and mortar or small food processor, crush coriander seeds and cumin seeds with peppercorns.

Add remaining ingredients and pound or mix to a smooth paste. Store in an airtight jar in refrigerator for up to four weeks.

Makes about 1/2 cup.

Note: The yield and hotness will vary according to the size and heat of the chiles.

RED CURRY PASTE

1 tablespoon coriander seeds
1 teaspoon cumin seeds
1 teaspoon peppercorns
4 garlic cloves, chopped
3 cilantro roots, chopped
8 dried red chiles, seeded, chopped
2 stalks lemon grass, chopped
Grated peel of 1/2 lime
1-1/4-inch piece galangal, chopped
2 teaspoons shrimp paste

Heat a wok, add coriander seeds and cumin seeds and heat until aroma changes. Using a pestle and mortar or small food processor, crush coriander and cumin seeds with peppercorns.

Add remaining ingredients and pound or mix to a smooth paste. Store in an airtight jar in refrigerator for up to 4 weeks.

Makes about 1/4 cup.

Note: The yield and hotness will vary according to the size and heat of the chiles.

—FRAGRANT CURRY PASTE—

2 garlic cloves, chopped
1 shallot, chopped
4 dried red chiles, seeded, chopped
1 thick stalk lemon grass, chopped
3 cilantro roots, chopped
Finely grated peel of 2 limes
1 kaffir lime leaf, torn
4 black peppercorns
1/2 teaspoon shrimp paste

Using a pestle and mortar or small food processor, pound or mix together garlic, shallot, chiles, lemon grass and cilantro roots.

Add lime peel, lime leaf, peppercorns and shrimp paste, and pound or mix to a smooth paste. Store in an airtight jar in the refrigerator for up to four weeks.

Makes about 6 tablespoons.

DIPPING SAUCE 1

1/2 cup tarmarind water, see page 13
1/2 to 3/4 teaspoon crushed palm sugar
1 or 2 drops fish sauce
1/2 teaspoon very finely chopped green onion
1/2 teaspoon very finely chopped garlic
1/2 teaspoon finely chopped fresh red chile

In a small saucepan, gently heat tarmarind water and sugar until sugar has dissolved.

Remove pan from heat. Add fish sauce, stir in green onion, garlic and chile. Pour into a small serving bowl and cool.

Makes 4 servings.

DIPPING SAUCE 2

6 tablespoons lime juice
1-1/2 to 2 teaspoons crushed palm sugar
1/2 teaspoon fish sauce
1/2 teaspoon very finely chopped shallot
1/2 teaspoon very finely chopped fresh green chile
1/2 teaspoon finely chopped fresh red chile

In a small bowl, stir together lime juice and sugar until sugar has dissolved. Adjust amount of sugar, if desired.

Stir in fish sauce, shallot and chile. Pour into a small serving bowl. Serve with deep-fried fish, fish fritters, won tons or spring rolls.

Makes 4 servings.

NAM PRIK

1 tablespoon fish sauce
About 22 whole dried shrimp, chopped
3 garlic cloves, chopped
4 dried red chiles with seeds, chopped
2 tablespoons lime juice
1 fresh red or green chile, seeded, chopped
About 1 tablespoon pea eggplant, if desired, chopped

Using a pestle and mortar or a small food processor, pound or mix together fish sauce, shrimp, garlic, dried chiles and lime juice to a paste.

Stir in fresh chile and eggplant, if using. Transfer to a small serving bowl.

Serve with a selection of raw vegetables. Store in an airtight jar in refrigerator several weeks.

Makes 6 to 8 servings.

——ROASTED NAM PRIK——

5 fresh red chiles
5 garlic cloves, unpeeled
5 shallots, unpeeled
1 tablespoon shrimp paste
1 tablespoon tamarind water, see page 13
2 teaspoons crushed palm sugar
2 tablespoons unsalted roasted peanuts

Preheat broiler. Broil chiles, garlic and shallots, turning occasionally, until skins are an even dark brown. Cool.

Peel garlic and shallots, then chop. Chop chiles; do not discard seeds. Using a pestle and mortar or a small food processor, pound or mix all ingredients to a paste.

Serve with cooked vegetables, salads, rice or fish. Store in an airtight jar in refrigerator up to a week.

Makes 6 servings.

LEMON GRASS SOUP

6 to 8 ounces raw shrimp
2 teaspoons vegetable oil
2-1/2 cups light fish stock
2 thick stalks lemon grass, finely chopped
3 tablespoons lime juice
1 tablespoon fish sauce
3 kaffir lime leaves, chopped
1/2 fresh red chile, thinly sliced
1/2 fresh green chile, thinly sliced
1/2 teaspoon crushed palm sugar
Cilantro leaves to garnish

Peel shrimp and remove dark veins running down their backs; reserve shrimp and shells.

In a wok, heat oil, add shrimp shells and fry, stirring occasionally, until they change color. Stir in stock, bring to a boil, reduce heat and simmer 20 minutes. Strain stock and return to wok; discard shells. Add lemon grass, lime juice, fish sauce, lime leaves, chiles and sugar. Simmer 2 minutes.

Add shrimp and cook just below simmering 2 to 3 minutes until shrimp are pink. Serve in heated bowls garnished with cilantro.

Makes 4 servings.

VERMICELLI SOUP

5 cups chicken stock
1 small onion, chopped
2 stalks lemon grass, chopped, crushed
2 kaffir lime leaves, shredded
1 tablespoon lime juice
3 garlic cloves, chopped
2 fresh red chiles, seeded, chopped
1-1/2-inch piece galangal, chopped
1-1/2 tablespoons fish sauce
2 teaspoons crushed palm sugar
4 ounces clear vermicelli, soaked in cold water
    10 minutes, drained
2 tablespoons coarsely chopped cilantro
Thai basil leaves to garnish

Put stock, onion, lemon grass, lime leaves, lime juice, garlic, chiles and galangal into a saucepan and simmer 20 minutes.

Stir in fish sauce and sugar. When sugar has dissolved, add vermicelli and cook 1 minute. Stir in cilantro. Spoon into warmed bowls and garnish with basil leaves.

Makes 4 to 6 servings.

CHICKEN & MUSHROOM SOUP

2 garlic cloves, crushed
4 cilantro sprigs
1-1/2 teaspoons peppercorns, crushed
1 tablespoon vegetable oil
4-1/2 cups chicken stock
5 pieces dried Chinese black mushrooms, soaked in
    cold water 30 minutes, drained, coarsely chopped
1 tablespoon fish sauce
4 ounces chicken, cut into strips
2 green onions, thinly sliced
Cilantro sprigs to garnish

Using a pestle and mortar or a small food processor, pound or mix garlic, 4 cilantro sprigs and peppercorns to a paste. In a wok, heat vegetable oil, add paste and cook, stirring, 1 minute. Stir in stock, mushrooms and fish sauce. Simmer 5 minutes.

Add chicken, reduce heat so liquid simmers and cook gently 5 minutes. Scatter green onions over surface and garnish with cilantro sprigs.

Makes 4 servings.

——PORK & PEANUT SOUP——

4 cilantro roots, chopped
2 garlic cloves, chopped
1 teaspoon peppercorns, cracked
1 tablespoon vegetable oil
8 ounces lean pork, very finely chopped
4 green onions, chopped
3 cups veal stock
2 ounces raw shelled peanuts
6 pieces dried black Chinese mushrooms, soaked 20
    minutes, drained and chopped
4 ounces bamboo shoots, coarsely chopped
1 tablespoon fish sauce

Using a pestle and mortar, pound to a paste cilantro roots, garlic and peppercorns.

In a wok, heat oil, add peppercorn paste and cook 2 to 3 minutes, stirring occasionally. Add pork and green onions and stir 1-1/2 minutes.

Stir stock, peanuts and mushrooms into wok, then cook at just below boiling 7 minutes. Add bamboo shoots and fish sauce and continue to cook 3 to 4 minutes.

Makes 3 to 4 servings.

—CHICKEN & COCONUT SOUP—

3-3/4 cups coconut milk
4 ounces boneless skinless chicken breast, cut into
  strips
2 stalks lemon grass, bruised and thickly sliced
2 green onions, thinly sliced
3 or 4 fresh red chiles, seeded, sliced
Juice of 1-1/2 limes
1 tablespoon fish sauce
1 tablespoon cilantro leaves, shredded
Cilantro leaves to garnish

Bring coconut milk to just below boiling. Add chicken and lemon grass.

Adjust heat so liquid simmers, then poach chicken, uncovered, until tender, about 4 minutes.

Add green onions and chiles. Heat briefly, then remove from heat and stir in lime juice, fish sauce and shredded cilantro. Garnish with cilantro leaves.

Makes 4 servings.

GOLD BAGS

4 ounces peeled cooked shrimp, finely chopped
2 ounces canned water chestnuts, finely chopped
2 green onions, white part only, finely chopped
1 teaspoon fish sauce
Freshly ground pepper
16 won-ton skins
Vegetable oil for deep-frying
Dipping Sauce 1, see page 21
Cilantro sprig to garnish

In a small bowl, mix together shrimp, water chestnuts, green onions, fish sauce and pepper.

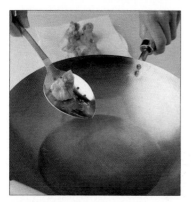

To shape each bag, put a small amount of shrimp mixture in center of each won-ton skin. Dampen edges of skins with a little water, then bring up over filling to form a bag. Press edges together to seal.

In a wok, heat oil to 375F (190C). Add bags in batches and fry about 2 to 3 minutes until crisp and golden. Using a slotted spoon, transfer to paper towels to drain. Serve hot with Dipping Sauce. Garnish with cilantro sprig.

Makes 16.

CORN CAKES

2 cups canned or cooked whole-kernel corn, drained
1 tablespoon Green Curry Paste, see page 18
2 tablespoons all-purpose flour
3 tablespoons rice flour
3 green onions, finely chopped
1 egg, beaten
2 teaspoons fish sauce
Vegetable oil for deep-frying
1-inch piece cucumber
Dipping Sauce 2, see page 22
1 tablespoon ground roasted peanuts

Place corn in a blender, add curry paste, all-purpose flour, rice flour, green onions, egg and fish sauce and mix together until corn is slightly chopped. Form into about 16 cakes. Heat oil in a wok to 350F (175C), then deep-fry one batch of corn cakes about 3 minutes until golden-brown.

Using a slotted spoon, transfer cakes to paper towels to drain. Keep warm in a warm oven while frying remaining cakes. Peel cucumber, quarter lengthwise, remove seeds and slice thinly. Place in a small bowl and mix in dipping sauce and ground peanuts. Serve with warm corn cakes.

Makes about 16.

— STUFFED CHICKEN WINGS —

4 large chicken wings
Small amount lean ground pork
1/4 cup cooked peeled shrimp, chopped
3 green onions, finely chopped
2 large garlic cloves, chopped
3 cilantro roots, chopped
2 tablespoons fish sauce
Freshly ground pepper
Vegetable oil for deep-frying
Rice flour for coating
Dipping Sauce 2, see page 22, to serve
Lettuce leaves to garnish

Bend wing joints backwards against joint. Using a small sharp knife or kitchen scissors, cut around top of bone that attaches wing to chicken body. Using blade of knife, scrape bone, turning back skin over unboned portion. Break bone free at joint.

Ease skin over joint and detach from flesh and bone. Working down the next bones, scrape off flesh and skin taking care not to puncture skin. Break bones free at joint, leaving end section.

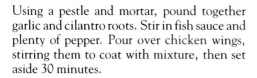

Chop chicken flesh from wings. Make up to 6 ounces (about 1 cup) with pork, if necessary. Place chicken and pork, if used, in a bowl and thoroughly mix together with shrimp and green onions. Stuff mixture into chicken wings; set aside.

Using a pestle and mortar, pound together garlic and cilantro roots. Stir in fish sauce and plenty of pepper. Pour over chicken wings, stirring them to coat with mixture, then set aside 30 minutes.

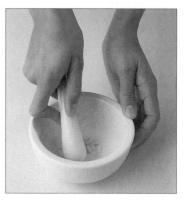

Heat oil in a wok to 350F (175C). Remove chicken wings from bowl, then toss in rice flour to coat completely. Add 2 at a time to oil and deep-fry 3 to 4 minutes until browned. Using a slotted spoon, transfer to paper towels to drain. Keep warm while frying remaining 2 chicken wings. Serve with sauce and garnish with lettuce leaves.

Makes 4 servings.

STEAMED EGGS

4 eggs, beaten
2 green onions, thinly sliced
3 ounces cooked peeled shrimp, finely chopped
Freshly ground pepper
1 red chile, seeded, thinly sliced
1 tablespoon cilantro leaves, chopped
1/3 cup coconut milk
2 teaspoons fish sauce
Cilantro sprigs and red chile rings to garnish

In a blender or a food processor, process all ingredients except cilantro sprigs until evenly blended.

Grease 4 individual heatproof dishes. Pour egg mixture into greased dishes. Place in a steaming basket, then place over a saucepan of boiling water. Cover and steam 10 to 12 minutes, until just set in center.

Remove from heat, let stand 1 or 2 minutes, then turn out onto a plate and invert onto a warmed plate. Garnish with cilantro sprigs and red chile rings.

Makes 2 to 4 servings.

STUFFED EGGS

4 eggs, at room temperature
1/4 cup ground cooked pork
1/4 cup finely chopped cooked shrimp
1 teaspoon fish sauce
1 garlic clove, chopped
1-1/2 tablespoons chopped cilantro
Finely ground pepper
Lettuce leaves to serve
Cilantro sprigs to garnish

Form 4 rings out of foil to hold eggs upright. Place in a steaming basket; set aside. Carefully place eggs into a saucepan of gently boiling water, cook 1-1/2 minutes, then remove with a slotted spoon.

Carefully peel a small part of the pointed end of each egg. With the point of a small sharp knife, cut a small hole down through the exposed white of each egg; reserve pieces of white that are removed. Pour liquid egg yolk and white from egg into a small bowl. Thoroughly mix in pork, shrimp, fish sauce, garlic, cilantro and pepper. Carefully spoon into eggs and replace removed pieces of white.

Set steaming basket over a saucepan of boiling water and place eggs, cut end uppermost, in foil 'rings'. Cover basket and steam eggs for about 12 minutes. When cool enough to handle, carefully peel off shells. Serve whole or halved on lettuce leaves, garnished with cilantro sprigs.

Makes 4 servings.

EGG NESTS

1 tablespoon chopped cilantro roots
1 garlic clove, chopped
1/2 teaspoon peppercorns, cracked
1 tablespoon peanut oil
1/2 small onion, finely chopped
4 ounces lean pork, very finely chopped
4 ounces peeled raw shrimp, chopped
2 teaspoons fish sauce
3 tablespoons vegetable oil
2 eggs
3 fresh red chiles, seeded, cut into thin strips
20 to 30 cilantro leaves
Cilantro sprigs to garnish

Using a pestle and mortar, pound together cilantro roots, garlic and peppercorns. In a wok, heat peanut oil, add peppercorn mixture and onion and stir-fry 1 minute.

Add pork, stir-fry 1 minute, then add shrimp. Stir-fry 45 seconds. Quickly stir in fish sauce, then transfer mixture to a bowl. Using paper towels, wipe out wok.

Add vegetable oil to wok and place over medium heat. In a small bowl, beat eggs. Spoon a small amount of beaten egg into a cone of waxed paper with a very small hole in the pointed end. Hold almost directly over wok, move above surface of wok, so trail of egg flows onto it and sets in threads. Quickly repeat, moving in another direction directly over threads. Repeat until there are 4 criss-crossed layers of egg.

Using a spatula, transfer nest to paper towels. Repeat with remaining eggs to make nests. Place nests with flat-side facing down. Place 2 chile strips to form a cross on each nest.

Top with cilantro leaves, then about 1 table-spoon of pork mixture. Fold nests over filling, turn over and arrange on serving plate. Garnish with cilantro sprigs.

Makes 4 servings.

SON-IN-LAW EGGS

Vegetable oil for deep-frying
6 eggs, hard-cooked and peeled
1 small onion, thinly sliced
2 tablespoons fish sauce
2 teaspoons palm sugar
1 fresh red chile, seeded, cut into thin slivers
Chile Flowers, see page 15, to garnish

Heat oil in a wok, add eggs and cook, turning occasionally, until golden-brown. Using a slotted spoon, transfer to paper towels to drain, then cut in half lengthwise. Place, cut-side up, on serving plates; set aside.

Pour all except 2 tablespoons of remaining oil from wok, add onion and fry until crisp and brown. Using a slotted spoon, transfer to paper towels; set aside.

Over low heat, stir together fish sauce, sugar and chile in wok, and continue to stir until sugar has melted. Simmer a few minutes until thickened. Add fried onions. When heated through, pour sauce over eggs and serve garnished with Chile Flowers.

Makes 6 servings.

——— PORK & NOODLE BALLS ———

3 garlic cloves, chopped
4 cilantro roots, chopped
1 cup ground lean pork (6 ounces)
1 small egg, beaten
2 teaspoons fish sauce
Freshly ground pepper
About 2 ounces egg thread noodles (1 coil)
vegetable oil for deep-frying
Dipping Sauce 1, see page 21, to serve

Using a pestle and mortar or small food processor, pound or mix together garlic and cilantro roots. In a bowl, mix together pork, egg, fish sauce and pepper, then stir in garlic mixture.

Place noodles in a heatproof strainer and dip in boiling water 5 seconds if fresh, or about 2 minutes if dried, until separated. Remove and rinse immediately under cold running water. Form pork mixture into about 12 balls. Neatly and evenly wind 3 or 4 strands of noodles around each ball to cover completely.

Heat oil in a wok to 350F (175C). Using a slotted spoon, lower 4 to 6 balls into oil and cook about 3 minutes until golden-brown and pork is cooked through. Using a slotted spoon, transfer to paper towels to drain. Keep warm while cooking remaining balls. Serve hot with Dipping Sauce.

Makes about 12 balls.

PORK TOASTS

6 ounces ground lean pork
1/4 cup finely chopped shrimp (2 ounces)
2 garlic cloves, chopped
1 tablespoon chopped cilantro
1-1/2 green onions, finely chopped
2 eggs, beaten
2 teaspoons fish sauce
Freshly ground pepper
4 day-old bread slices
1 tablespoon coconut milk
Vegetable oil for deep-frying
Cilantro leaves, thin red chile rings and cucumber
    slices to garnish

In a bowl, using a fork, mix together pork and shrimp, then thoroughly mix in garlic, cilantro, green onions, 1/4 of beaten eggs, the fish sauce and pepper. Divide mixture among bread slices, spreading it firmly to the edges. In a small bowl, stir together remaining eggs and coconut milk and brush over pork mixture. Trim crusts from bread, then cut each slice into rectangles.

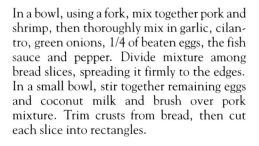

Heat oil in a wok to 375F (190C). Add several rectangles at a time, pork-side down, and fry 3 to 4 minutes until crisp, turning over after 2 minutes. Using a slotted spoon, transfer to paper towels to drain, then keep warm in a warm oven. Check temperature of oil after frying each batch. Serve warm garnished with cilantro leaves, chile rings and cucumber slices.

Makes 4 to 6 servings.

—————————STUFFED OMELET —————————

2 tablespoons vegetable oil
1 small onion, quartered, thinly sliced
3 garlic cloves, chopped
8 cilantro roots, chopped
14 peppercorns, cracked
5 ounces lean pork, very finely chopped
5 ounces long beans or green beans, thinly sliced, cut
    into 1-1/4-inch lengths
8 eggs, beaten
2 teaspoons fish sauce
1/4 cup chopped cilantro
Cilantro sprigs to garnish

Heat 1-1/2 tablespoons of the oil in a wok, add onion and cook, stirring occasionally, until lightly browned.

Using a pestle and mortar or small food processor, pound or mix together garlic, cilantro roots and peppercorns. Stir into wok and cook, stirring occasionally, 2 minutes. Add pork, stir-fry 2 minutes, then stir in beans. Stir-fry 2 minutes. Cover wok and set aside.

In a small bowl, mix eggs with fish sauce and chopped cilantro. In a skillet, heat remaining oil, pour in half of egg mixture and tilt pan to form a thin, even layer. Cook just until set. Spoon half of pork filling down center. Fold sides over filling to form a square package, then slide onto a warmed plate. Keep warm and repeat with remaining mixtures. Garnish with cilantro sprigs.

Makes 4 to 6 servings.

STEAMED CRAB

1 garlic clove, chopped
1 small shallot, chopped
Stems from 6 cilantro sprigs, finely chopped
6 ounces cooked crabmeat
4 ounces lean pork, very finely chopped, cooked
1 egg, beaten
1 tablespoon coconut cream, see page 11
2 teaspoons fish sauce
Freshly ground pepper
Cilantro leaves to garnish
1 red chile, seeded, cut into thin strips

Grease 4 individual heatproof dishes and place in a steaming basket.

Using a pestle and mortar, pound to a paste garlic, shallot and cilantro stems. In a bowl, stir together garlic paste, crabmeat, pork, egg, coconut cream, fish sauce and plenty of pepper until evenly mixed.

Divide among dishes, arrange cilantro leaves and chile strips on tops. Place steaming basket over a saucepan of boiling water and steam about 12 minutes until mixture is firm.

Makes 4 servings.

Note: Cleaned crab shells may be used instead of dishes for cooking.

STUFFED ZUCCHINI

2 ounces freshly grated coconut
6 tablespoons chopped cilantro
1 fresh green chile, seeded, finely chopped
4 zucchini (about 8 ounces each)
5 tablespoons vegetable oil
1 cup water
2 tablespoons lime juice
1 teaspoon crushed palm sugar
Freshly ground pepper
Few drops of fish sauce

In a small bowl, combine coconut, cilantro and chile; set aside.

Cut each zucchini crosswise into 4 pieces, each about 1-1/2 inches long. Stand each on a cut end and cut 2 deep slits like a cross, down 1 inch of the length. Gently pry apart cut sections and fill with coconut mixture. Pour oil and water into a wide skillet. Stand zucchini, filled-side up, in pan.

If any coconut mixture remains, sprinkle over zucchini. Sprinkle with lime juice, sugar, pepper and fish sauce. Heat to a simmer, cover tightly and simmer 5 to 6 minutes. Using two spoons, turn zucchini pieces over, re-cover and cook 7 to 10 minutes or until crisp-tender.

Makes 4 to 6 servings.

CRAB ROLLS

8 ounces cooked chicken, very finely chopped
4 ounces cooked crabmeat, flaked
4 green onions, finely chopped
1 ounce bean sprouts, finely chopped
1 small carrot, grated
2 teaspoons fish sauce
Freshly ground pepper
About 9 rice paper wrappers, each about 7 inches in diameter
Vegetable oil for deep-frying
Thai basil leaves, Thai mint leaves and lettuce leaves to serve
Dipping Sauce 1, see page 21

In a medium-size bowl, mix together chicken, crabmeat, green onions, bean sprouts, carrot, fish sauce and pepper. Brush both sides of each wrapper liberally with water and set aside to soften. Cut each into 4 wedges. Place a small amount of filling near wide end of one wedge, fold end over filling, tuck in sides and roll up. Repeat with remaining wedges and filling.

Preheat oil in a wok to 375F (190C). Fry rolls in batches 2 to 3 minutes until crisp and golden. Drain on paper towels. Serve hot. To eat, sprinkle each roll with herbs, then wrap in a lettuce leaf and dip into Dipping Sauce.

Makes 36.

FISH WITH GALANGAL

2 fresh red chiles, seeded, finely chopped
2 garlic cloves, finely chopped
1 shallot, finely chopped
1-1/2-inch piece galangal, finely chopped
2 stalks lemon grass, finely chopped
1 tablespoon fish sauce
20 Thai basil leaves
1 pound boneless firm white fish, such as halibut, cod
   or monkfish, cut into about 3/4-inch pieces
Banana leaves or foil

Using a pestle and mortar or small food processor, quickly mix together chiles, garlic,
shallot, galangal, lemon grass and fish sauce.
Turn into a bowl, stir in basil leaves and fish.
Divide among 3 or 4 pieces of banana leaf or
foil. Fold leaves or foil over fish to make neat
packages. Secure leaves with a wooden pick,
or fold foil edges tightly together.

Place in a steaming basket over boiling water
and steam about 7 minutes until fish is just
cooked.

Makes 3 to 4 servings.

—FISH WITH LEMON GRASS—

2 tablespoons vegetable oil
1 flat fish, such as sole or flounder (about 1-1/2 pounds), ready to cook
4 garlic cloves, finely chopped
2 fresh red chiles, seeded, finely chopped
1 shallot, chopped
4-1/2 tablespoons lime juice
1/2 teaspoon crushed palm sugar
1-1/2 tablespoons finely chopped lemon grass
2 teaspoons fish sauce
Chile Flower, see page 15, to garnish

In a wok, heat oil, add fish, skin-side down first, and cook 3 to 5 minutes per side until lightly browned and flesh is opaque when tested with a knife. Using a spatula, transfer to a warmed platter, cover and keep warm. Add garlic to wok and fry, stirring occasionally, until browned.

Stir in chiles, shallot, lime juice, sugar, lemon grass and fish sauce. Simmer 1 to 2 minutes. Pour over the fish and garnish with Chile Flower.

Makes 2 servings.

FISH WITH CILANTRO & GARLIC

6 cilantro roots, chopped
3 large garlic cloves, chopped
5 peppercorns, crushed
2 fish fillets, such as trout or flounder
2 pieces banana leaf or foil
3 tablespoons lime juice
1/2 teaspoon crushed palm sugar
1 green onion, finely chopped
1/2 small green chile seeded, thinly sliced
1/2 small red chile, seeded, thinly sliced
Chile Flowers, see page 15, to garnish

Preheat broiler. Using a pestle and mortar or small food processor, pound or mix together cilantro roots, garlic and peppercorns. Spread evenly over inside of fish fillets, then let stand 30 minutes.

Wrap fish in banana leaves or pieces of foil, securing leaf with wooden pick, or folding edges of foil tightly together. Broil about 8 minutes. Meanwhile, in a small bowl, stir together lime juice and sugar, then stir in green onion and chiles. Serve with fish. Garnish with Chile Flowers.

Makes 2 servings.

FISH WITH MUSHROOM SAUCE

About 1/2 cup all-purpose flour
Salt and freshly ground pepper
1 flat fish, such as sole or flounder (about 1-1/2
    pounds), ready to cook
2 tablespoons vegetable oil plus oil for deep-frying
3 garlic cloves, thinly sliced
1 small onion, halved and thinly sliced
1-3/4-inch piece gingerroot, finely chopped
4 ounces shiitake mushrooms, sliced
2 teaspoons fish sauce
1/2 cup water
3 green onions, sliced
Green Onion Brushes, see page 14, to garnish

Season flour with salt and pepper, then use to lightly dust fish. Heat oil for deep-frying in a large deep skillet to 350F (175C), add fish and cook 4 to 5 minutes, turning halfway through, until crisp and browned.

Meanwhile, heat the 2 tablespoons oil in a wok, add garlic, onion and gingerroot and cook, stirring occasionally, 2 minutes. Add mushrooms and stir-fry 2 minutes. Stir in fish sauce, water and green onions. Bring to a boil. Using a spatula, transfer fish to paper towels to drain. Put on a warmed serving plate and spoon sauce over fish. Garnish with Green Onion Brushes.

Makes 2 servings.

——FISH IN COCONUT SAUCE——

4 tablespoons vegetable oil
1 shallot, chopped
1-1/2-inch piece galangal, finely chopped
2 stalks lemon grass, finely chopped
1 small fresh red chile, seeded, chopped
1/2 cup coconut milk
2 teaspoons fish sauce
5 cilantro sprigs
About 12 ounces white fish fillets, such as halibut or
    red snapper
1 small onion, sliced
Freshly ground pepper

In a wok, heat 1 tablespoon of the oil over high heat, add shallot, galangal, lemon grass and chile. Stir 3 minutes until lightly colored. Transfer to a small food processor, add coconut milk, fish sauce and cilantro stems (reserve leaves) and process until mixed. Place fish in a heatproof, shallow, round dish. Pour coconut mixture over fish. Cover dish, place over saucepan of boiling water and steam 8 to 10 minutes until fish is opaque when tested with a knife.

Meanwhile, heat remaining oil in a wok over medium heat, add onion and cook, stirring occasionally, until browned. Using a slotted spoon, transfer to paper towels. Add reserved cilantro leaves to oil and fry a few seconds. Using a slotted spoon, transfer to paper towels to drain. Scatter fried onions and cilantro leaves over fish and season with plenty of pepper.

Makes 3 to 4 servings.

FISH WITH TAMARIND & GINGER

6 tablespoons vegetable oil
1 (2-1/2-lb.) whole fish or 1 single piece, such as cod,
　　bass or red snapper
1 small onion, finely chopped
6 green onions, thickly sliced
2 garlic cloves, crushed
1 tablespoon grated gingerroot
2 teaspoons fish sauce
1-1/2 tablespoons light soy sauce
1 teaspoon crushed palm sugar
1 tablespoon tamarind water, see page 13
Freshly ground pepper
Cilantro sprigs to garnish

Over medium heat, heat 4 tablespoons of the oil in a wok. Add fish and fry about 5 minutes on each side, until browned and flesh is opaque when tested with a knife. Meanwhile, heat remaining oil in a small saucepan over medium heat, add onion and cook, stirring occasionally, until browned. When fish is cooked, drain on paper towels. Arrange fish on a platter and keep warm.

Stir into wok the green onions, garlic and gingerroot. Stir-fry 2 to 3 minutes, then stir in fish sauce, soy sauce, sugar and tamarind water. Cook 1 minute, season with pepper, then pour over fish. Sprinkle fish with browned onions and garnish with cilantro sprigs.

Makes 4 servings.

FISH WITH CHILE SAUCE

1 flat fish, such as flounder or sole (about 1-1/2
  pounds), ready to cook
2 teaspoons vegetable oil plus oil for brushing
3 small dried red chiles, halved lengthwise
2 garlic cloves, finely chopped
1 teaspoon fish sauce
1/3 cup tamarind water, see page 13
1 teaspoon crushed palm sugar

Preheat broiler. Brush fish lightly with oil, then broil about 4 minutes per side until lightly colored and flesh is opaque when tested with a knife. Using a spatula, transfer to a warmed platter and keep warm.

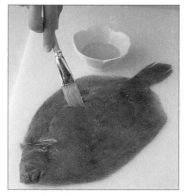

In a small pan, heat the 2 teaspoons vegetable oil, add chiles and garlic and cook 1 minute. Stir in remaining ingredients and simmer 2 to 3 minutes until lightly thickened. Spoon over fish.

Makes 2 servings.

—FISH IN BANANA LEAF CUPS—

3 ounces firm white fish, such as cod or hake, very
    finely chopped
3 ounces peeled shrimp, very finely chopped
2 to 3 teaspoons Red Curry Paste, see page 19
2 tablespoons ground roasted peanuts
1 kaffir lime leaf, finely chopped
2 tablespoons coconut milk
1 egg
2 teaspoons fish sauce
Leafy part of 1/2 Chinese cabbage leaf, finely shredded
2 Banana Leaf Cups, see page 16, if desired
2 teaspoons coconut cream, see page 11
Red chile strips to garnish

In a bowl, using a fork, mix fish and shrimp
together. Mix in curry paste, peanuts and
lime leaf. In a small bowl, mix together coconut milk, egg and fish sauce. Stir into fish
mixture to evenly combine; set aside 30
minutes.

Divide cabbage leaf among banana cups or
heatproof individual dishes to make a thin
layer. Stir fish mixture and divide among cups
or dishes. Place in a steaming basket and
steam over a saucepan of boiling water. Cover
pan and steam about 15 minutes until just set
in center. Place on a serving plate, drizzle
coconut cream over top and garnish with
chile strips.

Makes 2 servings.

—SHRIMP IN YELLOW SAUCE—

2 fresh red chiles, seeded, chopped
1 red onion, chopped
1 thick stalk lemon grass, chopped
1-inch piece galangal, chopped
1 teaspoon ground turmeric
1/2 cup water
1 cup coconut milk
14 to 16 raw large shrimp, peeled, deveined
8 Thai basil leaves
2 teaspoons lime juice
1 teaspoon fish sauce
1 green onion, including some green top, cut into thin
  strips

Using a small food processor, mix to a paste chiles, red onion, lemon grass and galangal. Transfer to a wok and heat, stirring, 2 to 3 minutes, then stir in turmeric and water and bring to a boil. Reduce heat and simmer 3 to 4 minutes until most of the water has evaporated.

Stir in coconut milk and shrimp and simmer, stirring occasionally, about 4 minutes until shrimp are just firm and pink. Stir in basil leaves, lime juice and fish sauce. Sprinkle green onion over shrimp.

Makes 4 servings.

——— SHRIMP WITH GARLIC ———

2 tablespoons vegetable oil
5 garlic cloves, chopped
1/4-inch slice gingerroot, very finely chopped
14 to 16 large shrimp, peeled, tails on, deveined
2 teaspoons fish sauce
2 tablespoons chopped cilantro
1 to 2 tablespoons water
Freshly ground pepper
Lettuce leaves, lime wedges and diced cucumber to
　　serve

In a wok, heat oil, add garlic and fry until browned.

Stir in gingerroot, heat 30 seconds, then add shrimp and stir-fry 2 to 3 minutes until beginning to turn pink. Stir in fish sauce, cilantro, water and plenty of pepper. Boil 1 to 2 minutes.

Line a plate with lettuce; top with shrimp. Serve with lime wedges and diced cucumber.

Makes 4 servings.

– DEEP-FRIED COCONUT SHRIMP –

1-1/2-inch piece cucumber
Dipping Sauce 1, see page 21
Leaves from 1 cilantro sprig, chopped
8 uncooked jumbo shrimp
Vegetable oil for deep-frying
BATTER:
4 ounces rice flour
3 tablespoons unsweetened shredded coconut
1 egg, separated
3/4 cup coconut milk
1 teaspoon fish sauce

Cut cucumber into quarters lengthwise, remove and discard seeds, then thickly slice. Place in a small bowl and add Dipping Sauce. Stir in cilantro; set aside. Peel shrimp, leaving tails on. Cut along back of each one and remove black vein. Set shrimp aside. Preheat oil in a wok to 350F (175C).

For batter, in a small bowl, stir together flour and coconut. Gradually stir in egg yolk, coconut milk and fish sauce. In another small bowl, beat egg white until stiff but not dry; fold into batter. Dip shrimp in batter; add to hot oil in batches. Cook 2 to 3 minutes until golden. Using a slotted spoon, transfer to paper towels to drain. Keep warm while frying remaining shrimp. Serve shrimp with sauce.

Makes 3 to 4 servings.

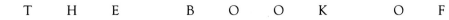

— STIR-FRIED SHRIMP & GINGER —

3 garlic cloves, crushed
1-1/2-inch piece gingerroot, thinly sliced
2 tablespoons vegetable oil
12 to 16 raw large shrimp, peeled, tails on, deveined
2 shallots, finely chopped
Grated peel of 1/2 lime
2 teaspoons fish sauce
3 tablespoons water
3 green onions, thinly sliced
Lime juice to serve
Green Onion Brushes, see page 14, to garnish

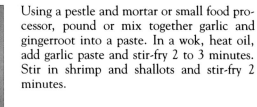

Using a pestle and mortar or small food processor, pound or mix together garlic and gingerroot into a paste. In a wok, heat oil, add garlic paste and stir-fry 2 to 3 minutes. Stir in shrimp and shallots and stir-fry 2 minutes.

Stir in lime peel, fish sauce and water. Boil 1 minute until shrimp are pink. Stir in green onions, then remove from heat. Serve in a warm dish sprinkled with lime juice and garnished with onion brushes.

Makes 3 to 4 servings.

——— SCALLOPS WITH LIME ———

12 scallops in half-shells
1 tablespoon vegetable oil
2 garlic cloves, chopped
1 shallot, finely chopped
1/4-inch slice galangal, finely chopped
1 teaspoon finely chopped fresh red chile
3 tablespoons lime juice
1/4 teaspoon crushed palm sugar
1 teaspoon fish sauce
Shredded cilantro leaves to garnish

Lay scallops in their shells in a steaming basket.

Heat oil in a wok, add garlic and shallot and cook, stirring occasionally, until softened. Add galangal; stir 1 minute. Sprinkle mixture over scallops. Cover steaming basket and place over a wok or saucepan of boiling water and steam 6 to 8 minutes until scallops just begin to turn opaque.

In a saucepan over low heat, cook chile, lime juice, sugar and fish sauce until sugar dissolves. Transfer scallops in their shells to a plate, spoon lime sauce over scallops and sprinkle with cilantro.

Makes 3 to 4 servings.

—SHRIMP WITH MUSHROOMS—

1 dried red chile, seeded, soaked in hot water 20
   minutes, drained and chopped
1-1/4-inch piece gingerroot, chopped
2 garlic cloves, chopped
2 shallots, chopped
1 stalk lemon grass, chopped
1 tablespoon fish sauce
15 to 20 Thai basil leaves
16 large raw shrimp, peeled, tails on, deveined
2 to 3 large shiitake mushrooms, thinly sliced

Using a pestle and mortar or small food processor, pound or mix together chile, gingerroot, garlic, shallots and lemon grass. Stir in
fish sauce and basil leaves.

Place shrimp in a shallow heatproof bowl and
spoon spice mixture over to coat evenly. Add
mushrooms. Or, wrap shrimp and mushrooms
in a banana leaf and secure with wooden
picks. Place bowl or banana leaf package in a
steamer above boiling water, cover and cook
about 8 minutes until shrimp are pink.

Makes 3 to 4 servings.

MUSSELS WITH BASIL

1-1/2 pounds mussels in shells, cleaned, debearded and
   rinsed
1 large garlic clove, chopped
3-inch piece galangal, thickly sliced
2 stalks lemon grass, chopped
10 Thai basil sprigs
1 tablespoon fish sauce
Thai basil leaves to garnish
Dipping Sauce 2, see page 22, to serve

Place mussels, garlic, galangal, lemon grass,
basil sprigs and fish sauce in a large saucepan.
Add water to a depth of 1/2 inch. Cover pan,
bring to a boil and cook about 5 minutes,
shaking pan frequently, until mussels have
opened. Discard any mussels that remain
closed.

Transfer mussels to a large warmed bowl or
individual bowls, and strain cooking liquid
over mussels. Garnish with basil leaves.
Serve with sauce for dipping.

Makes 2 to 3 servings.

— SHRIMP & CUCUMBER CURRY —

1/4 cup coconut cream, see page 11
3 to 4 tablespoons Red Curry Paste, see page 19
8 ounces raw large peeled shrimp
8-inch length cucumber, halved lengthwise, seeded, cut
    into 3/4-inch pieces
1-1/4 cups coconut milk
2 tablespoons tamarind water, see page 13
1 teaspoon crushed palm sugar
Cilantro leaves to garnish

In a wok, heat coconut cream, stirring, until it boils and thickens, and the oil begins to separate. Add the curry paste, and cook, stirring, 3 minutes. Stir in shrimp to coat, then stir in cucumber. Add coconut milk, tamarind water and sugar.

Simmer 3 to 4 minutes until shrimp are pink. Transfer to a warmed serving dish and garnish with cilantro.

Makes 3 servings.

DUCK CURRY

5 tablespoons coconut cream, see page 11
5 tablespoons Green Curry Paste, see page 18
1 (3-lb.) duck, skinned if desired, trimmed of excess
    fat, divided into 8 portions
2-1/2 cups coconut milk
1 tablespoon fish sauce
8 kaffir lime leaves, shredded
2 fresh green chiles, seeded, thinly sliced
12 Thai basil leaves
Leaves from 5 cilantro sprigs
Cilantro sprigs to garnish

Heat coconut cream in a wok over medium heat, stirring, until it thickens and the oil begins to separate.

Stir in curry paste and cook about 5 minutes until mixture darkens. Stir in duck pieces to coat with curry mixture. Reduce heat, cover and cook 15 minutes, stirring occasionally. Stir in coconut milk, fish sauce and lime leaves. Heat to a simmer, then cook without boiling, turning duck over occasionally, 30 to 40 minutes until meat is very tender. Remove surplus fat from the surface, then stir in chiles.

Cook 5 minutes. Stir in basil and cilantro leaves and cook 2 minutes. Garnish with cilantro sprigs.

Makes 4 servings.

—CHICKEN IN COCONUT MILK—

8 peppercorns
6 cilantro roots, finely chopped
1-3/4-inch piece galangal, thinly sliced
2 fresh green chiles, seeded, thinly sliced
2-1/2 cups coconut milk
Grated peel and juice of 1 lime
4 kaffir lime leaves, shredded
1 (3-lb.) chicken, cut into 8 pieces
1 tablespoon fish sauce
3 tablespoons chopped cilantro leaves to serve

Using a pestle and mortar or small food processor, crush peppercorns, then add cilantro roots and galangal and pound or mix lightly together.

In a wok, briefly heat peppercorn mixture, stirring, then stir in chiles, coconut milk, lime peel and lime leaves. Bring to a simmer, add chicken and simmer 40 to 45 minutes until chicken is very tender and liquid is reduced.

Stir in fish sauce and lime juice. Scatter cilantro leaves over chicken and serve.

Makes 6 to 8 servings.

CHICKEN WITH CILANTRO

6 cilantro sprigs
1 tablespoon peppercorns
2 garlic cloves, chopped
Juice of 1 lime
2 teaspoons fish sauce
4 large or 6 medium-size chicken drumsticks or thighs
Lime wedges to serve
Green Onion Brushes, see page 14, to garnish

Using a pestle and mortar or small food processor, pound or mix together cilantro, peppercorns, garlic, lime juice and fish sauce; set aside.

Using the point of a sharp knife, cut slashes in chicken. Spread spice mixture over chicken; cover and refrigerate 2 to 3 hours, turning occasionally.

Preheat broiler. Broil chicken, basting and turning occasionally, about 10 minutes until golden and cooked through. Serve with lime wedges and garnish with Green Onion Brushes.

Makes 2 to 3 servings.

LEMON GRASS CHICKEN CURRY

12 ounces boneless chicken, chopped into small pieces
1 tablespoon Red Curry Paste, see page 19
3 tablespoons vegetable oil
2 garlic cloves, finely chopped
1 tablespoon fish sauce
2 stalks lemon grass, finely chopped
5 kaffir lime leaves, shredded
1/2 teaspoon crushed palm sugar
1/2 cup water

Place chicken in a bowl, add curry paste and stir to coat chicken; set aside 30 minutes.

In a wok, heat oil, add garlic and fry until golden. Stir in chicken, then fish sauce, lemon grass, lime leaves, sugar and water.

Simmer 15 to 20 minutes until chicken is cooked through. If chicken becomes too dry, add a little more water, but the final dish should be quite dry.

Makes 3 to 4 servings.

BARBECUED CHICKEN

4 fresh red chiles, seeded, sliced
2 garlic cloves, chopped
5 shallots, finely sliced
2 teaspoons crushed palm sugar
1/2 cup coconut cream, see page 11
2 teaspoons fish sauce
1 tablespoon tamarind water, see page 13
4 skinless boneless chicken breasts
Thai basil leaves or cilantro leaves to garnish

Using a pestle and mortar or small food processor, pound or mix together chiles, garlic and shallots to a paste. Work in sugar, then stir in coconut cream, fish sauce and tamarind water.

Using the point of a sharp knife, cut 4 slashes in each chicken breast. Place chicken in a shallow dish and pour spice mixture over chicken. Turn to coat, cover dish and set aside 1 hour.

Preheat broiler. Place chicken on a piece of foil and broil about 4 minutes per side, basting occasionally, until cooked through.

Makes 4 servings.

SPICED CHICKEN

5 shallots, chopped
3 garlic cloves, chopped
5 cilantro roots, chopped
2 stalks lemon grass, chopped
2 fresh red chiles, seeded, chopped
1-1/2-inch piece gingerroot, finely chopped
1 teaspoon shrimp paste
1-1/2 tablespoons vegetable oil
2 chicken legs, divided into thighs and drumsticks
1-1/2 tablespoons tamarind water, see page 13
1/3 cup water

Using a pestle and mortar, pound to a smooth paste shallots, garlic, cilantro roots, lemon grass, chiles, gingerroot and shrimp paste.

Heat oil in a wok, stir in shallot mixture and cook, stirring 3 to 4 minutes. Stir in chicken pieces to coat evenly.

Add tamarind water and water. Cover and simmer about 30 minutes until chicken is tender. If chicken becomes too dry, add a little more water.

Makes 3 to 4 servings.

CHICKEN WITH BASIL

2 tablespoons vegetable oil
2 garlic cloves, chopped
12 ounces skinless boneless chicken breasts, finely chopped
1 small onion, finely chopped
3 fresh red chiles, seeded, thinly sliced
20 Thai basil leaves
1 tablespoon fish sauce
1/4 cup coconut milk
Squeeze of lime juice
Chile Flowers, see page 15, and Thai basil leaves to garnish

In a wok, heat 1 tablespoon of the oil, add garlic, chicken, onion and chiles and cook, stirring occasionally, 3 to 5 minutes until cooked through.

Stir in basil leaves, fish sauce and coconut milk. Stir briefly over heat. Add lime juice. Garnish with Chile Flowers and basil leaves.

Makes 2 to 3 servings

—CHICKEN WITH GALANGAL—

1 pound boneless skinless chicken breasts
3 tablespoons vegetable oil
2 garlic cloves, finely chopped
1 onion, quartered, sliced
1-inch piece galangal, finely chopped
8 pieces dried Chinese black mushrooms, soaked 30
    minutes, drained and chopped
1 fresh red chile, seeded, cut into thin strips
1 tablespoon fish sauce
1-1/2 teaspoons crushed palm sugar
1 tablespoon lime juice
12 Thai mint leaves
4 green onions, including some green tops, chopped
3 to 4 tablespoons water
Thai mint leaves to garnish

Using a sharp knife, cut chicken into 2-1/2-inch-long × 1-inch-wide pieces; set aside. In a wok, heat oil, add garlic and onion and cook, stirring occasionally, until golden. Stir in chicken and stir-fry about 2 minutes.

Add galangal, mushrooms and chile and stir-fry 1 minute. Stir in fish sauce, sugar, lime juice, mint leaves, green onions and water. Cook, stirring, about 1 minute. Transfer to a warmed dish and garnish with mint leaves.

Makes 4 servings.

—CHICKEN IN PEANUT SAUCE—

1-inch piece galangal, chopped
2 garlic cloves, chopped
1-1/2 tablespoons Fragrant Curry Paste, see page 20
1/4 cup coconut cream, see page 11
1 pound boneless skinless chicken breasts, cut into
   large pieces
2 tablespoons vegetable oil
3 shallots, chopped
1/4 cup roasted peanuts, chopped
2 cups coconut milk
1/2 teaspoon finely chopped dried red chile
2 teaspoons fish sauce
Freshly cooked broccoli to serve

Using a pestle and mortar or small food processor, pound or mix together galangal, garlic and curry paste. Mix in coconut cream. Place chicken in a bowl and stir in spice mixture; set aside 1 hour.

In a wok, heat the oil, add shallots and coated chicken and stir-fry 3 to 4 minutes. In a blender, mix peanuts with coconut milk, then stir into chicken with chile and fish sauce. Simmer about 30 minutes until chicken is tender and sauce is thickened. Transfer to center of a warmed plate and arrange broccoli around chicken.

Makes 4 servings.

—CHICKEN WITH SNOW PEAS—

3 tablespoons vegetable oil
3 garlic cloves, chopped
1 dried red chile, seeded, chopped
3 shallots, chopped
2 tablespoons lime juice
2 teaspoons fish sauce
1/4 cup water
12 ounces chicken, finely chopped
1-1/2 stalks lemon grass, chopped
1 kaffir lime leaf, chopped
6 ounces snow peas
1-1/2 tablespoons coarsely ground browned rice, see
    page 13
3 green onions, chopped
Chopped cilantro leaves to garnish

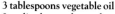

In a wok, heat 2 tablespoons of the oil, add garlic and cook, stirring occasionally, until lightly browned. Stir in chile, shallots, lime juice, fish sauce and water. Simmer 1 to 2 minutes, then stir in chicken, lemon grass lime leaf, fish sauce and water. Cook, stirring, for 2 to 3 minutes until chicken is just cooked through. Transfer to a warmed plate and keep warm.

Heat remaining oil in wok, add snow peas and stir-fry for 2 to 3 minutes until just tender. Transfer to a warmed serving plate. Return chicken to wok. Add rice and green onions. Heat for about 1 minute, then transfer to serving plate. Garnish with chopped cilantro.

Makes 3-4 servings.

— STEAMED CHICKEN CURRY —

1 recipe Fragrant Curry Paste, see page 20
1-1/3 cups coconut milk
5 tablespoons water
1 pound boneless skinless chicken breasts, sliced
4 kaffir lime leaves, shredded
8 Thai basil leaves
Thai basil sprig to garnish

Using a small food processor, mix together curry paste, 1/3 cup of the coconut milk and the water; set aside. Place chicken in a heat-proof bowl or dish, stir in remaining coconut milk and set aside 30 minutes.

Stir curry-flavored coconut milk, lime leaves and basil leaves into chicken, cover top tightly with foil and place in a steaming basket.

Cover and place over a saucepan of boiling water. Steam about 40 minutes until chicken is tender. Garnish with basil sprig.

Makes 4 to 5 servings.

Note: In Thailand the curry is steamed on a bed of lettuce and basil leaves, wrapped in a banana leaf.

–CHICKEN WITH LEMON GRASS–

1 (3-lb.) chicken, cut into 8 pieces
4 large stalks lemon grass
4 green onions, chopped
4 peppercorns, cracked
2 tablespoons vegetable oil
1 fresh green chile, seeded and thinly sliced
1/4 cup water
2 teaspoons fish sauce
1 fresh red chile, seeded and cut into thin slivers to
    garnish

With the point of a sharp knife, cut slashes in each chicken piece; place in a shallow dish.

Bruise top parts of each lemon grass stalk and reserve. Chop lower parts, then pound with green onions and peppercorns using a pestle and mortar. Spread over chicken and into slashes. Cover and let stand 2 hours.

In a wok, heat oil, add chicken and cook turning occasionally, about 5 minutes until lightly browned. Add green chile, bruised lemon grass stalks and water. Cover wok and cook slowly 25 to 30 minutes, until chicken is cooked through. Stir in fish sauce. Transfer chicken pieces to a warmed serving dish, add cooking juices and sprinkle with red chile.

Makes 4 to 6 servings.

BEEF CURRY

2 tablespoons vegetable oil
3 tablespoons Red Curry Paste, see page 19
12 ounces lean beef, cut into cubes
1 stalk lemon greass, finely chopped
4 ounces long beans, or green beans, cut into
    1-1/2-inch lengths
About 8 pieces dried Chinese black mushrooms,
    soaked 20 minutes, drained and chopped
3 tablespoons roasted peanuts
1 fresh green chile, seeded and chopped
1/4 cup water
1 tablespoon fish sauce
2 teaspoons crushed palm sugar
15 Thai mint leaves

In a wok, heat the oil, add curry paste and stir
3 minutes. Add beef and lemon grass and stir-
fry 5 minutes. Add beans and mushrooms,
stir-fry 3 minutes then stir in peanuts and
chile.

Stir for 1 minute then stir in water, fish sauce
and sugar and cook about 2 minutes until
beans are crisp-tender. Transfer to a warmed
serving dish and sprinkle with mint leaves.

Makes 3-4 servings.

PORK WITH WATER CHESTNUTS

1-1/2 tablespoons vegetable oil
4 garlic cloves, chopped
2 fresh red chiles, seeded, finely chopped
12 ounces lean pork, cubed
10 water chestnuts, chopped
1 teaspoon fish sauce
1/4 cup water
Freshly ground pepper
3 tablespoons chopped cilantro
6 green onions, chopped
3 to 4 Green Onion Brushes, see page 14, to garnish

In a wok, heat oil, add garlic and chiles and cook, stirring occasionally, until garlic is golden.

Stir in pork and stir-fry about 2 minutes until almost cooked through. Add water chestnuts, heat 2 minutes, then stir in fish sauce, water and add plenty of pepper. Stir in cilantro and green onions. Garnish with Green Onion Brushes.

Makes 3 to 4 servings.

BARBECUED SPARERIBS

2 tablespoons chopped cilantro stems
3 garlic cloves, chopped
1 teaspoon peppercorns, cracked
1 teaspoon grated lime peel
1 tablespoon Green Curry Paste, see page 18
2 teaspoons fish sauce
1-1/2 teaspoons crushed palm sugar
3/4 cup coconut milk
2 pounds pork spareribs, trimmed
Green Onion Brushes, see page 14, to garnish

Using a pestle and mortar or small food processor, pound or mix together cilantro, garlic, peppercorns, lime peel, curry paste, fish sauce and sugar. Stir in coconut milk. Place spareribs in a shallow dish, pour spiced coconut mixture over ribs, cover and refrigerate 3 hours, basting occasionally.

Preheat a barbecue or a moderate broiler. Cook ribs about 10 minutes per side until cooked through and browned, basting occasionally with coconut mixture. Garnish with Green Onion Brushes.

Makes 4 to 6 servings.

Note: The ribs can also be cooked on a rack in a roasting pan in an preheated 400F (205C) oven 45 to 60 minutes, basting occasionally.

──── PORK & BEAN STIR-FRY ────

2 tablespoons vegetable oil
6 garlic cloves, chopped
12 ounces lean pork, finely chopped
12 ounces long beans or small green beans
12 water chestnuts, sliced
4 ounces cooked peeled shrimp
1 tablespoon fish sauce
1/2 teaspoon crushed palm sugar
Freshly ground pepper
About 3 tablespoons water

In a wok, heat oil, add garlic and fry, stirring occasionally, until golden.

Add pork and beans and stir-fry 2 minutes, then add water chestnuts.

Stir 1 minute, then add shrimp, fish sauce, sugar, plenty of pepper and water. Boil 1 to 2 minutes, then transfer to a warmed serving plate.

Makes 4 servings.

──────── THAI PORK CURRY ────────

1/2 cup coconut cream, see page 11
1 onion, chopped
1 garlic cloves, finely crushed
2 tablespoons Fragrant Curry Paste, see page 20
2 teaspoons fish sauce
1/2 teaspoon crushed palm sugar
12 ounces lean pork, diced
3 kaffir lime leaves, shredded
25 Thai basil leaves
1 long fresh red chile, seeded, cut into strips, and Thai basil sprigs, to garnish

In a wok, heat 1/3 cup of the coconut cream until the oil begins to separate. Stir in onion and garlic and cook, stirring occasionally, until lightly browned. Stir in curry paste and cook, stirring, about 2 minutes. Stir in fish sauce and sugar, then add pork and stir to coat. Cook 3 to 4 minutes.

Add lime leaves and basil leaves and cook 1 minute. If necessary, add a little water, but final dish should be dry. Drizzle remaining coconut cream over finished dish and garnish with chile strips and basil sprigs.

Makes 3 servings.

PORK SATAY

12 ounces lean pork, cubed
Juice of 1 lime
1 stalk lemon grass, finely chopped
1 garlic clove, finely chopped
2 tablespoons vegetable oil
SAUCE:
4 tablespoons vegetable oil
1/2 cup raw shelled peanuts
2 stalks lemon grass, chopped
2 fresh red chiles, seeded, sliced
3 shallots, chopped
2 garlic cloves, chopped
1 teaspoon fish paste
2 tablespoons crushed palm sugar
1-1/2 cups coconut milk
Juice of 1/2 lime

Divide pork among 4 skewers and lay in a shallow dish. In a bowl, mix together lime juice, lemon grass, garlic and oil. Pour over pork, turn to coat, cover and refrigerate 1 hour, turning occasionally.

Preheat broiler. Remove pork from dish, allowing excess liquid to drain off. Broil pork, turning frequently and basting, 8 to 10 minutes.

Meanwhile, make sauce. Over a high heat, heat 1 tablespoon of the oil in a wok, add nuts and cook, stirring constantly, 2 minutes. Using a slotted spoon, transfer nuts to paper towels to drain. Using a pestle and mortar or small food processor, grind nuts to a paste. Remove and set aside.

Using a pestle and mortar or small food processor, pound or mix to a smooth paste lemon grass, chiles, shallots, garlic and fish paste.

Heat remaining oil in wok, add spice mixture and cook, stirring, 2 minutes. Stir in peanut paste, sugar and coconut milk. Bring to a boil, stirring. Reduce heat so sauce simmers, add lime juice and simmer, stirring, 5 to 10 minutes, until thickened. Serve in a bowl to accompany pork. Garnish with Carrot Flowers, see page 17, and lettuce leaves.

Makes 4 servings.

—PORK & BAMBOO SHOOTS—

2 tablespoons vegetable oil
4 garlic cloves, very finely chopped
12 ounces lean pork, very finely chopped
4 ounces whole bamboo shoots, sliced crosswise
1/4 cup peanuts, coarsely chopped
2 teaspoons fish sauce
Freshly ground pepper
4 large green onions, thinly sliced
Thai basil leaves to garnish

In a wok, heat oil, add garlic and fry, stirring occasionally, about 3 minutes until lightly colored.

Add pork and stir-fry 2 minutes. Add bamboo shoots and cook 1 minute.

Stir in peanuts, fish sauce, plenty of pepper and half of the green onions. Transfer to a warmed serving plate and sprinkle with remaining green onions and the basil leaves.

Makes 4 servings.

VEGETABLES & PORK

8 ounces lean pork, very finely chopped
Freshly ground pepper
2 tablespoons vegetable oil
3 garlic cloves, finely chopped
1 pound prepared mixed vegetables, such as snow peas,
    broccoli, red bell pepper and zucchini
1 tablespoon fish sauce
1/2 teaspoon crushed palm sugar
1 cup water
3 green onions, finely chopped

In a bowl, mix together pork and plenty of pepper. Set aside 30 minutes.

In a wok or skillet, heat oil, add garlic, cook, stirring occasionally, 2 to 3 minutes, then stir in pork.

Stir briefly until pork changes color. Stir in vegetables, then fish sauce, sugar and water. Stir 3 to 4 minutes until snow peas are bright green and vegetables are crisp-tender. Stir in green onions.

Makes 4 servings.

—PORK WITH GREEN ONIONS—

2-1/2 cups coconut milk
1 pound lean pork, cut into 1-inch cubes
1 tablespoon fish sauce
1/2 teaspoon crushed palm sugar
1 cup raw shelled peanuts, skins removed
3 fresh red chiles, seeded, chopped
1-1/2-inch piece galangal, chopped
4 garlic cloves
1 stalk lemon grass, chopped
1/4 cup coconut cream, see page 11
8 green onions, chopped
2 pounds spinach
Warmed coconut cream, see page 11, and roasted
    peanuts to serve

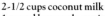

In a wok, heat coconut milk to a simmer, lower heat so liquid barely moves, add pork and cook about 25 minutes until very tender. Meanwhile, using a small food processor mix fish sauce, sugar, raw peanuts, chiles, galangal, garlic and lemon grass to a paste. In another wok or a skillet, heat coconut cream until the oil separates. Add green onions and peanut paste and cook, stirring frequently, 2 to 3 minutes.

Stir in milk from pork and boil until slightly thickened. Pour over pork, stir and cook 5 minutes more. Rinse spinach leaves, then pack into a pan with just water left on them. Gently cook about 3 minutes until just warmed. Arrange on a warmed serving plate. Spoon pork and sauce onto center. Drizzle with warmed coconut cream and sprinkle with roasted peanuts.

Makes 4 to 6 servings.

—NOODLES, PORK & SHRIMP—

7 ounces bean thread noodles
6 dried Chinese black mushrooms
2 tablespoons vegetable oil
12 ounces lean pork, very finely chopped
4 ounces peeled cooked large shrimp
3 shallots, finely chopped
4 green onions, including some green tops, sliced
3 small inner celery stalks, thinly sliced
2 ounces dried shrimp
2 tablespoons fish sauce
5 tablespoons lime juice
1-1/2 teaspoons crushed palm sugar
2 fresh red chiles, seeded, chopped
1/4 cup cilantro leaves, chopped
Whole cooked shrimp and cilantro leaves to garnish

Soak noodles 15 minutes, then drain. Meanwhile soak mushrooms in water 30 minutes. Drain and chop. In a wok, heat oil, add pork and stir-fry 2 to 3 minutes until cooked through. Using a slotted spoon, transfer to paper towels. Add noodles to a pan of boiling water and boil 5 minutes. Drain well and set aside.

Cut each large shrimp into 3 pieces, place in a bowl and add shallots, green onions, celery, mushrooms, noodles, pork and dried shrimp. Toss together. In a small bowl, mix together fish sauce, lime juice, sugar and chiles. Add cilantro leaves and toss ingredients together. Serve garnished with shrimp and cilantro leaves.

Makes 4 servings.

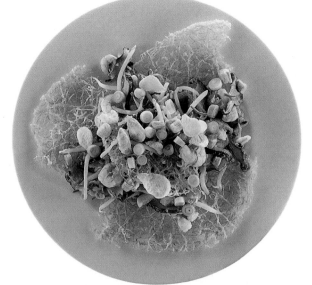

CRISPY NOODLES

6 ounces rice vermicelli
6 pieces dried Chinese black mushrooms
4 ounces lean pork
4 ounces chicken breast
Vegetable oil for deep-frying
2 eggs
4 garlic cloves, finely chopped
3 shallots, thinly sliced
1 fresh red chile, seeded and sliced
1 fresh green chile, seeded and sliced
6 tablespoons lime juice
1 tablespoon fish sauce
1 tablespoon crushed palm sugar
1-1/2 ounces peeled cooked shrimp
4 ounces bean spouts
3 green onions, thickly sliced

Soak vermicelli in water 20 minutes, then drain and set aside. Soak mushrooms in water 20 minutes, drain, chop and set aside. Cut pork and chicken into cubes or 1-inch strips. Set aside.

For garnish, heat 2 teaspoons vegetable oil in a wok. In a small bowl, beat eggs with 2 tablespoons water, then drip small amounts in batches in tear shapes onto wok. Cook 1-1/2 to 2 minutes until set. Remove using a thin spatula. Set aside.

Add enough oil to wok for deep-frying. Heat to 375F (190C). Add noodles in batches and fry until puffed, light golden-brown and crisp. Transfer to paper towels. Set aside.

Pour off oil leaving 3 tablespoons. Add garlic and shallots and cook, stirring occasionally, until lightly browned. Add pork, stir-fry 1 minute, then stir in chicken and stir-fry 2 minutes. Stir in chiles, mushrooms, lime juice, fish sauce and sugar.

Boil until liquid becomes slightly syrupy. Add shrimp, bean sprouts and noodles, tossing to coat with sauce without breaking up noodles. To serve, garnish with green onions and egg tear shapes.

Makes 4 servings.

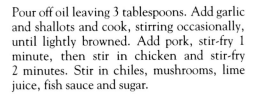

THAI FRIED NOODLES

3 tablespoons vegetable oil
4 garlic cloves, finely crushed
1 tablespoon fish sauce
3 to 4 tablespoons lime juice
1 teaspoon crushed palm sugar
2 eggs, beaten
12 ounces rice vermicelli, soaked in water 20 minutes, drained
4 ounces peeled shrimp
4 ounces bean sprouts
4 green onions, sliced
2 tablespoons dried shrimp, ground, to garnish
Finely chopped roasted peanuts, cilantro leaves and lime slices to garnish

Heat oil in a wok, add garlic and cook, stirring occasionally, until golden. Stir in fish sauce, lime juice and sugar until sugar has dissolved. Quickly stir in eggs and cook for a few seconds. Stir in noodles to coat with garlic and egg, then add shrimps, 3/4 of the bean sprouts and half of the green onions.

When noodles are tender, transfer contents of wok to a warmed serving dish. Garnish with remaining bean sprouts and green onions, dried shrimp, peanuts, cilantro leaves and lime slices.

Makes 4 servings.

—NOODLES WITH HERB SAUCE—

1/2 cup vegetable oil
2 tablespoons raw shelled peanuts
1 small green chile, seeded, sliced
3/4-inch piece galangal, chopped
2 large garlic cloves, chopped
Leaves from 1 bunch Thai basil (about 90)
Leaves from 1 small bunch Thai mint (about 30)
Leaves from 1 small bunch cilantro (about 45)
2 tablespoons lime juice
1 teaspoon fish sauce
12 to 16 ounces egg noodles, soaked 5 to 10 minutes

Over high heat, heat oil in a wok, add pea-nuts and cook, stirring, about 2 minutes, until browned. Using a slotted spoon, trans-fer nuts to paper towels to drain; reserve oil.

Using a small food processor, coarsely grind peanuts. Add chile, galangal and garlic. Mix briefly. Add herbs, lime juice, fish sauce and reserved oil. Drain noodles, shake to loosen, then cook in boiling salted water 2 minutes, until soft. Drain well, turn into a warmed dish and toss with sauce.

Makes 4 servings.

–NOODLES, CRAB & EGGPLANT–

8 ounces dark and white crabmeat
6 ounces dried egg thread noodles
3 tablespoons vegetable oil
1 eggplant (about 8 ounces), cut into about 2-inch x
    1/4-inch strips
2 garlic cloves, very finely chopped
1/2-inch slice galangal, finely chopped
1 fresh green chile, finely chopped
6 green onions, sliced
1 tablespoon fish sauce
2 teaspoons lime juice
1-1/2 tablespoons chopped cilantro leaves

In a bowl, mash well dark crabmeat. Coarsely
mash white crabmeat; set aside.

Add noodles to a pan of boiling salted water
and cook about 4 minutes until just tender.
Drain well. Meanwhile, in a wok, heat 2
tablespoons of the oil, add eggplant and stir-
fry about 5 minutes until evenly browned.
Using a slotted spoon, transfer to paper
towels; set aside.

Add remaining oil to wok, heat, then one by
one stir in garlic, galangal, chile and green
onions. Add noodles, toss together 1 minute,
then toss in crabmeat and eggplant. Sprinkle
with fish sauce, lime juice and cilantro and
toss to mix. Garnish with cilantro leaves.

Makes 3 servings.

— NOODLES WITH BROCCOLI —

8 ounces broccoli
2 tablespoons vegetable oil
3 garlic cloves, finely chopped
8 ounces lean pork, finely chopped
1 pound fresh rice noodles or 8 ounces egg thread
   noodles
1/4 cup roasted peanuts, chopped
2 teaspoons fish sauce
1/2 teaspoon crushed palm sugar
3 tablespoons water
1 fresh red chile, seeded and cut into thin slivers to
   garnish

Cut broccoli diagonally into 1/2-inch-wide pieces and cook in boiling salted water 2 minutes. Drain, refresh under cold running water and drain well; set aside.

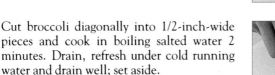

Heat oil in a wok, add garlic and fry, stirring occasionally, until golden. Using a slotted spoon, transfer to paper towels; set aside. Add pork to wok and stir-fry 2 minutes. Add noodles, stir quickly, then add broccoli and peanuts and stir-fry 2 minutes. Stir in fish sauce, sugar and water. Stir briefly and serve garnished with reserved garlic and chile slivers.

Makes 4 servings.

—RICE, SHRIMP & BEAN CURD—

3/4 cup long-grain white rice
3 tablespoons vegetable oil
3 garlic cloves, chopped
1 small onion, chopped
4 ounces bean curd, drained and cut into about
    1/2-inch cubes
2 fresh small red chiles, seeded, finely chopped
1 tablespoon fish sauce
6 ounces peeled shrimp
1 shallot, thinly sliced
Chile Flower, see page 15, unpeeled cooked shrimp and
    cilantro leaves to garnish

Cook rice, see page 12. In a wok, heat oil, add garlic and onion and cook, stirring occasionally, 3 to 4 minutes until lightly browned. Add bean curd and fry about 3 minutes until browned. Add chiles and stir-fry briefly. Stir in fish sauce and rice; cook, stirring, 2 to 3 minutes, then stir in shrimp.

Add shallot, stir quickly to mix, then transfer rice mixture to a warmed serving dish. Garnish with Chile Flower, shrimp and cilantro leaves.

Makes 4 servings.

SPICY FRIED RICE

3/4 cup long-grain white rice
2 tablespoons vegetable oil
1 large onion, finely chopped
3 garlic cloves, chopped
2 fresh green chiles, seeded, finely chopped
2 tablespoons Red Curry Paste, see page 19
2 ounces lean pork, very finely chopped
3 eggs, beaten
1 tablespoon fish sauce
1/3 cup cooked peeled shrimp
Thinly sliced red chile, shredded cilantro leaves and
    Green Onion Brushes, see page 14, to garnish

Cook rice, see page 12. Heat oil in a wok, add onion, garlic and chiles and cook, stirring occasionally, until onion has softened. Stir in curry paste and cook, stirring, 4 minutes. Add pork and stir-fry 2 to 3 minutes. Stir in rice to coat with ingredients, then push to side of wok.

Pour eggs into center of wok. When just beginning to set, stir into the rice, adding fish sauce at the same time. Stir in shrimp, then transfer rice mixture to a warmed serving dish and garnish with chile, cilantro and onion brushes.

Makes 4 servings.

THAI FRIED RICE

3/4 cup long-grain white rice
4 ounces long beans or green beans, cut into 1-inch
   lengths
3 tablespoons vegetable oil
2 onions, finely chopped
3 garlic cloves, crushed
3 ounces lean pork, very finely chopped
3 ounces boneless skinless chicken breast, very finely
   chopped
2 eggs, beaten
2 tablespoons Nam Prik, see page 23
1 tablespoon fish sauce
3 ounces cooked peeled shrimp
Cilantro leaves, shredded
Green onions and lime wedges to garnish

Cook rice, see page 12. Add beans to a pan
of boiling water and cook 2 minutes. Drain
and refresh under cold running water. Drain
well. In a wok, heat oil, add onions and garlic
and cook, stirring occasionally, until softened. Stir in pork and chicken and stir-fry 1
minute. Push to side of wok.

Pour eggs into center of wok. When just
beginning to set, stir in pork mixture followed by Nam Prik, fish sauce and rice. Stir 1 to
2 minutes, then add beans and shrimp.
Garnish with cilantro leaves, green onions
and lime wedges.

Makes 4 servings.

RICE, CHICKEN & MUSHROOMS

3/4 cup long-grain white rice
2 tablespoons vegetable oil
1 small onion, finely chopped
2 garlic cloves, finely chopped
2 fresh red chiles, seeded, cut into slivers
8 ounces boneless skinless chicken breasts, finely
   chopped
3 ounces bamboo shoots, chopped
8 pieces dried Chinese black mushrooms, soaked 30
   minutes, drained and chopped
2 tablespoons dried shrimp
1 tablespoon fish sauce
About 25 Thai basil leaves
Thai basil leaves to garnish

Cook rice, see page 12. Heat oil in a wok, add onion and garlic and cook, stirring occasionally, until golden. Add chiles and chicken and stir-fry 2 minutes.

Stir in bamboo shoots, mushrooms, dried shrimp and fish sauce. Stir-fry 2 minutes, then stir in rice and the 25 basil leaves. Garnish with additional basil leaves.

Makes 4 servings.

STUFFED EGGPLANT

2 eggplant (each about 8 ounces)
2 garlic cloves, finely chopped
2 stalks lemon grass, chopped
2 tablespoons vegetable oil
1 small onion, finely chopped
6 ounces boneless skinless chicken breasts, finely
   chopped
2 teaspoons fish sauce
25 Thai basil leaves
Freshly ground pepper
Thai basil leaves to garnish

Preheat broiler. Place eggplant under broiler
and cook, turning as necessary, about 20
minutes until evenly charred.

Meanwhile, using a pestle and mortar, pound
together garlic and lemon grass; set aside.
Heat oil in a wok, add onion and cook, stirring occasionally, until lightly browned. Stir
in garlic mixture, cook 1 to 2 minutes, then
add chicken. Stir-fry 2 minutes. Stir in fish
sauce, the 25 basil leaves and plenty of
pepper.

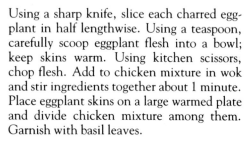

Using a sharp knife, slice each charred eggplant in half lengthwise. Using a teaspoon,
carefully scoop eggplant flesh into a bowl;
keep skins warm. Using kitchen scissors,
chop flesh. Add to chicken mixture in wok
and stir ingredients together about 1 minute.
Place eggplant skins on a large warmed plate
and divide chicken mixture among them.
Garnish with basil leaves.

Makes 4 servings.

──── STIR-FRIED SNOW PEAS ────

2 tablespoons vegetable oil
3 garlic cloves, finely chopped
4 ounces lean pork, very finely chopped
1 pound snow peas
1/2 teaspoon crushed palm sugar
1 tablespoon fish sauce
2 ounces cooked peeled shrimp, chopped
Freshly ground pepper

Heat oil in a wok over medium heat, add garlic and fry until lightly colored. Add pork and stir-fry 2 to 3 minutes.

Add snow peas and stir-fry about 3 minutes until crisp-tender.

Stir in sugar, fish sauce, shrimp and pepper. Heat briefly.

Makes 4 servings.

—— BROCCOLI WITH SHRIMP ——

3 tablespoons peanut oil
4 garlic cloves, finely chopped
1 red chile, seeded, thinly sliced
1 pound trimmed broccoli, cut diagonally into 1-inch
   slices
4 ounces cooked shrimp
1 tablespoon fish sauce
1/2 teaspoon crushed palm sugar
Chile Flowers, see page 15, to garnish

Heat oil in a wok, add garlic and fry, stirring occasionally, until just beginning to color. Add chile and cook 2 minutes.

Quickly stir in broccoli. Stir-fry 3 minutes. Reduce heat, cover wok and cook 4 to 5 minutes until broccoli is crisp-tender.

Remove lid and stir in shrimp, fish sauce and sugar. Garnish with Chile Flowers.

Makes 4 servings.

SPICED CABBAGE

14 peppercorns
2 tablespoons coconut cream, see page 11
2 shallots, chopped
4 ounces lean pork, finely chopped
About 1 pound white cabbage, finely sliced
1-1/4 cups coconut milk
1 tablespoon fish sauce
1 fresh red chile, very finely chopped

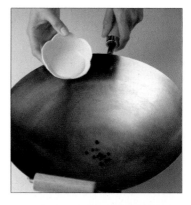

In a wok, heat peppercorns about 3 minutes, until aroma changes. Stir in coconut cream, heat 2 to 3 minutes, then stir in shallots.

Stir-fry 2 to 3 minutes, then stir in pork and cabbage. Cook, stirring occasionally, 3 minutes. Add coconut milk and bring just to a boil. Reduce heat, cover and simmer 5 minutes.

Uncover and cook about 10 minutes until cabbage is crisp-tender. Stir in fish sauce. Sprinkle with chopped chile.

Makes 4 to 5 servings.

—VEGETABLES WITH SAUCE—

1 eggplant (about 8 ounces)
4 ounces long beans or green beans
3 ounces cauliflowerets
2 cups coconut milk
2 shallots, chopped
2 garlic cloves, chopped
4 cilantro roots, chopped
2 dried red chiles, seeded, chopped
2 stalks lemon grass, chopped
1-1/4-inch piece galangal, chopped
Grated peel of 1 lime
1/4 cup coconut cream, see page 11
1-1/2 tablespoons ground roasted peanuts
3 tablespoons tamarind water, see page 13
1 tablespoon fish sauce
2 teaspoons crushed palm sugar

Cut eggplant into 1-1/2-inch cubes; cut beans into 2-inch lengths. Put all vegetables into a pan, add coconut milk and bring to a boil. Cover and simmer 10 minutes until vegetables are tender. Remove from heat, uncover and set aside. Using a pestle and mortar or small food processor, pound or mix together shallots, garlic, cilantro roots, chiles, lemon grass, galangal and lime peel.

Mix in 1/4 cup liquid from vegetables. Place in a small, heavy skillet, stir in coconut cream and heat, stirring, until the oil separates and paste is thick. Stir into vegetables with peanuts, tamarind water, fish sauce and sugar. Simmer about 1 minute.

Makes 6 servings.

MUSHROOMS & BEAN SPROUTS

2 tablespoons vegetable oil
2 fresh red chiles, seeded, thinly sliced
2 garlic cloves, chopped
8 ounces shiitake mushrooms, sliced
4 ounces bean sprouts
4 ounces cooked peeled shrimp
2 tablespoons lime juice
2 shallots, sliced crosswise
1 tablespoon fish sauce
1/2 teaspoon crushed palm sugar
1 tablespoon ground browned rice, see page 13
6 cilantro sprigs, stems and leaves finely chopped
10 Thai mint leaves, shredded
Thai mint leaves to garnish

Heat oil in a wok, add chiles and garlic and cook, stirring occasionally, 2 to 3 minutes. Add mushrooms and stir-fry 2 to 3 minutes.

Add bean sprouts and shrimp, stir-fry 1 minute, then stir in lime juice, shallots, fish sauce and sugar. When hot, remove from heat and stir in rice, cilantro and shredded mint. Garnish with mint leaves.

Makes 4 servings.

TOSSED SPINACH

2 tablespoons peanut oil
8 ounces chicken, very finely chopped
6 garlic cloves, finely chopped
1-1/2 pounds spinach leaves, torn into large pieces
1-1/2 tablespoons fish sauce
Freshly ground pepper
1-1/2 tablespoons dry-fried unsalted peanuts, chopped
Thinly sliced fresh red chile, to garnish

Heat oil in a wok, add chicken and stir-fry 2 to 3 minutes. Using a slotted spoon, transfer to paper towels; set aside.

Add garlic to wok and fry until just colored. Using a slotted spoon, transfer 1/2 of the garlic to paper towels; set aside. Increase heat beneath wok so oil is lightly smoking. Quickly add spinach, stir briefly to coat with oil and garlic.

Top spinach with chicken and sprinkle with fish sauce and pepper. Reduce heat, cover wok and simmer 2 to 3 minutes. Scatter peanuts and reserved garlic on top and garnish with sliced chile. Serve immediately.

Makes 4 servings.

——CHICKEN & MINT SALAD——

1 stalk lemon grass, finely chopped
2 to 3 chiles, seeded, finely chopped
3 tablespoons lime juice
1 tablespoon fish sauce
2 teaspoons crushed palm sugar
1-1/2 tablespoons vegetable oil
1 pound boneless skinless chicken breasts, very finely
    chopped
15 Thai mint leaves, shredded
Lettuce leaves to serve
Mint leaves and Chile Flowers, see page 15, to garnish

In a bowl, mix together lemon grass, chiles,
lime juice, fish sauce and sugar; set aside.

Heat oil in a wok, stir in chicken and cook
over medium-high heat, stirring, about 1-1/2
minutes until cooked through. Using a
slotted spoon, quickly transfer to paper
towels to drain and add to bowl with chile
mixture.

Add mint and toss lightly. Line a plate with
lettuce leaves; spoon chicken mixture into
center. Garnish with mint leaves and Chile
Flowers.

Makes 4 servings.

CUCUMBER SALAD

2 tablespoons vegetable oil
2 tablespoons raw shelled peanuts
1 large cucumber, peeled
1 fresh small red chile, seeded, thinly sliced
1 fresh small green chile, seeded, thinly sliced
1 shallot, finely chopped
2 teaspoons finely chopped lime peel
1-1/2 tablespoons lime juice
2 teaspoons fish sauce
1 teaspoon crushed palm sugar
About 15 dried shrimp, finely chopped

Heat oil in a wok until very hot, add peanuts
and cook, stirring, 2 to 3 minutes until lightly
browned.

Using a slotted spoon, transfer to paper
towels to drain; set aside. Cut cucumber in
half lengthwise, scoop out and discard seeds.
Cut into small chunks and place in a bowl; set
aside.

Mix together chiles, shallot, lime peel, lime
juice, fish sauce and sugar. Pour over cucumber and toss lightly. Chop peanuts and scatter
over cucumber with chopped shrimp.

Makes 3 to 4 servings.

— SHRIMP SALAD WITH MINT —

16 to 20 raw large shrimp, peeled, deveined
Juice of 2 limes
2 teaspoons vegetable oil
2 teaspoons crushed palm sugar
2 tablespoons tamarind water, see page 13
1 tablespoon fish sauce
2 teaspoons Red Curry Paste, see page 19
2 stalks lemon grass, very finely chopped
1/4 cup coconut cream, see page 11
5 kaffir lime leaves, shredded
10 Thai mint leaves, shredded
1 small crisp lettuce head, divided into leaves
1 small cucumber, thinly sliced
Thai mint leaves to garnish

Put shrimp in a bowl, add lime juice and let stand 30 minutes. Remove shrimp, allowing any excess liquid to drain into a bowl; reserve liquid. Heat oil in a wok, add shrimp and stir-fry 2 to 3 minutes until just cooked. (Marinating in lime juice partially cooks them.)

Meanwhile, stir sugar, tamarind water, fish sauce, curry paste, lemon grass, coconut cream, lime leaves and mint leaves into reserved lime liquid. Stir in cooked shrimp. Cover and refrigerate until cold. Line a plate with lettuce; top with a layer of cucumber slices. Spoon shrimp and dressing on top. Garnish with mint leaves.

Makes 3 to 4 servings.

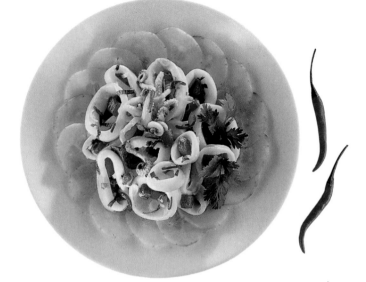

SQUID SALAD

1 pound small or medium-size squid
2 tablespoons vegetable oil
1/2 small red bell pepper, halved lengthwise
1 tablespoon fish sauce
3 tablespoons lime juice
1 teaspoon crushed palm sugar
2 garlic cloves, very finely crushed
1 stalk lemon grass, very finely chopped
1 red chile, seeded, thinly sliced
10 Thai mint leaves, shredded
2 tablespoons chopped cilantro
2 green onions, finely chopped
1 cucumber, peeled, if desired, and thinly sliced
Cilantro sprigs to garnish

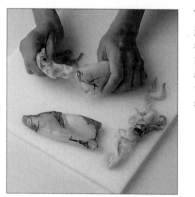

To clean squid, hold head just below eyes and gently pull away from body pouch. Discard soft viscera that come away with it. Carefully remove ink sac; retain if desired. Pull quill-shaped pen free from pouch and discard. Slip your fingers under skin on body pouch, and slip it off.

Cut off edible fins on either side of pouch. Cut off tentacles just below eyes; discard head. Squeeze out beak-like mouth from in among the tentacles and discard. Rinse tentacles, pouch and fins thoroughly, dry well, then slice into rings.

Heat oil in a wok, add squid and fry gently, stirring occasionally 10 to 15 minutes, until tender. Using a slotted spoon, transfer to paper towels to drain.

Meanwhile, preheat broiler, then broil bell pepper, turning frequently, 8 to 10 minutes until evenly charred. Let cool enough to handle, then remove skin and coarsely chop.

In a bowl, mix together fish sauce, lime juice, sugar and garlic. Add squid and toss together, then toss with lemon grass, chile, bell pepper, mint, cilantro and green onions. Arrange cucumber slices on a plate. Place the squid salad on cucumber and garnish with cilantro sprigs.

Makes 3 to 4 servings.

Variation: Instead of cucumber, serve with small inner celery stalks.

THAI BEEF SALAD

12 ounces lean beef, very finely chopped
1-1/2 tablespoons long-grain rice, browned and
    coarsely ground, see page 13
1 tablespoon fish sauce
2 tablespoons lime juice
2 teaspoons crushed palm sugar
2 fresh green chiles, seeded, finely chopped
2 garlic cloves, finely chopped
8 Thai mint leaves
4 kaffir lime leaves, torn
8 Thai basil leaves
Lettuce leaves to serve
Chopped green onions and a Chili Flower, see page 15,
    to garnish

Heat a wok, add beef and dry-fry about 2 minutes until no longer pink. Transfer to a bowl. In a small bowl, mix together ground rice, fish sauce, lime juice and sugar. Pour over warm beef and toss together. Cover and cool until slightly warm.

Add chiles, garlic and mint, lime leaves and basil leaves to bowl and toss ingredients together. Line a plate with lettuce leaves; spoon beef mixture into center. Top with green onions and garnish with Chile Flower.

Makes 3 to 4 servings.

PORK & BAMBOO SHOOT SALAD

3 tablespoons vegetable oil
3 garlic cloves, chopped
1 small onion, thinly sliced
8 ounces lean pork, very finely chopped
1 egg, beaten
1 (8-oz.) can bamboo shoots, drained, cut into strips
1 tablespoon fish sauce
1 teaspoon crushed palm sugar
3 tablespoons lime juice
Freshly ground pepper
Lettuce leaves to serve
Fried garlic and onion to garnish

In a wok, heat 2 tablespoons of the oil, add garlic and onion and cook, stirring occasionally, until lightly browned. Using a slotted spoon, transfer to paper towels to drain; set aside. Add pork to wok and stir-fry about 3 minutes until cooked through. Using a slotted spoon, transfer to paper towels; set aside. Using paper towels, wipe out wok.

Heat remaining oil in wok, pour in egg to make a thin layer and cook 1 to 2 minutes until just set. Turn over and cook 1 minute. Remove, roll up and cut into strips. In a bowl, toss together pork, bamboo shoots and egg. In a small bowl, stir together fish sauce, sugar, lime juice and plenty of pepper. Pour over pork mixture and toss. Line a plate with lettuce leaves; spoon pork mixture into center. Sprinkle with fried garlic and onion.

Makes 3 to 4 servings.

——CHICKEN & WATERCRESS——

2 garlic cloves, finely chopped
1-1/4-inch piece galangal, finely chopped
1 tablespoon fish sauce
3 tablespoons lime juice
1 teaspoon crushed palm sugar
2 tablespoons peanut oil
8 ounces chicken, very finely chopped
About 25 dried shrimp
1 bunch watercress (about 4 ounces), coarse stalks
    removed
3 tablespoons chopped roasted peanuts
2 fresh red chiles, seeded, cut into thin strips

Using a pestle and mortar, pound together garlic and galangal. Mix in fish sauce, lime juice and sugar; set aside. In a wok, heat oil, add chicken and stir-fry about 3 minutes until cooked through. Using a slotted spoon, transfer to paper towels to drain, then put into a serving bowl. Set aside.

Chop half the dried shrimp and add to bowl with chicken. Mix in watercress, peanuts and half of the chiles. Add garlic mixture and toss to mix. Sprinkle with remaining chiles and shrimp.

Makes 3 to 4 servings.

—HOT BAMBOO SHOOT SALAD—

1 tablespoon fish sauce
2 tablespoons tamarind water, see page 13
1/2 teaspoon crushed palm sugar
1 garlic clove, finely chopped
1 small fresh red chile, seeded, finely chopped
2 tablespoons water
6 ounces bamboo shoots, cut into thin strips
1 tablespoon coarsely ground browned rice, see page 13
2 green onions, including some green tops, sliced
Cilantro leaves to garnish

In a pan, bring fish sauce, tamarind water, sugar, garlic, chile and water to a boil. Stir in bamboo shoots and heat 1 to 2 minutes.

Stir in rice, then turn into a serving dish, top with green onions and garnish with cilantro leaves.

Makes 2 to 3 servings.

BEAN SALAD

2 tablespoons lime juice
2 tablespoons fish sauce
1/2 teaspoon crushed palm sugar
1-1/2 tablespoons Nam Prik, see page 23
2 tablespoons ground roasted peanuts
2 tablespoons water
2 tablespoons vegetable oil
3 garlic cloves, finely chopped
3 shallots, thinly sliced
1/4 dried red chile, seeded, finely chopped
2 tablespoons coconut cream, see page 11
8 ounces long beans or green beans, very thinly sliced

In a small bowl, mix together lime juice, fish sauce, sugar, Nam Prik, peanuts and water; set aside. In a small saucepan, heat oil, add garlic and shallots and cook, stirring occasionally, until beginning to brown. Stir in chile and cook until garlic and shallots are browned. Using a slotted spoon, transfer to paper towels; set aside.

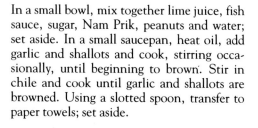

In a small saucepan over low heat, warm coconut cream, stirring occasionally. Bring a medium-size saucepan of water to a boil, add beans, return to a boil and cook about 30 seconds. Drain and refresh under cold water. Drain well. Transfer to a serving bowl and toss with shallot mixture and contents of small bowl. Drizzle warm coconut cream over top.

Makes 3 to 4 servings.

COCONUT CREPES

4 ounces rice flour
1/3 cup sugar
Pinch of salt
1-3/4 cups shredded coconut
2 eggs, beaten
2-1/2 cups coconut milk
Green food coloring and red food coloring, if desired
Vegetable oil for cooking
Tangerine sections, to serve, if desired

In a bowl, stir together rice flour, sugar, salt and coconut.

Form a well in center, add eggs, then gradually draw in flour mixture, slowly pouring in coconut milk at same time, to make a smooth batter. If desired, divide batter evenly among 3 bowls. Stir green food coloring into one bowl to color batter pale green; color another batch pink and leave remaining batch plain. Heat a 6-inch crepe or omelet pan over medium heat, swirl around a little oil, then pour off excess. Stir batter well, then add 2 to 3 spoonfuls to pan.

Rotate to cover bottom, then cook over medium heat about 4 minutes until lightly browned underneath and set. Carefully turn over and cook briefly on other side. Transfer to a warmed plate and keep warm while cooking remaining batter. Serve rolled up with tangerine sections, if using.

Makes about 10.

Note: The mixture is delicate so the first 2 or 3 crepes may be difficult to make perfectly.

— MANGO WITH STICKY RICE —

1-1/4 cups sticky rice, soaked overnight in cold water
1 cup coconut milk
Pinch of salt
2 to 4 tablespoons sugar or to taste
2 large ripe mangoes, peeled and halved
3 tablespoons coconut cream, see page 11
Mint leaves to decorate

Drain and rinse rice thoroughly. Place in a steaming basket lined with a double thickness of cheesecloth. Steam over simmering water 30 minutes. Remove from heat.

In a medium-size bowl, stir together coconut milk, salt and sugar to taste until sugar has dissolved. Stir in warm rice. Set aside 30 minutes.

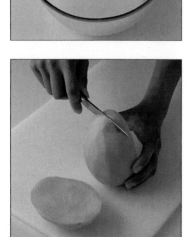

Thinly slice mangoes by cutting lengthwise through flesh to the seed. Discard the seeds. Spoon rice into mounds in centers of 4 plates and arrange mango slices around. Pour coconut cream over rice. Decorate with mint leaves.

Makes 4 servings.

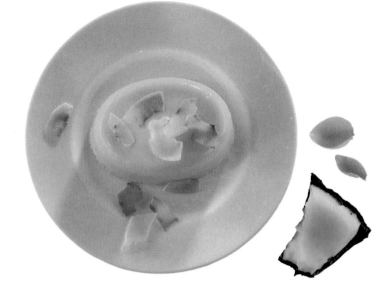

COCONUT CUSTARDS

2 egg yolks
3 eggs
2 cups coconut milk
1/3 cup sugar
Few drops rosewater or jasmine extract
Toasted coconut to decorate

Preheat oven to 350F (175C). Place 4 individual heatproof custard cups in a baking pan.

In a medium-size bowl, stir together egg yolks, eggs, coconut milk, sugar and rosewater or jasmine extract until sugar dissolves. Pour through a strainer into cups. Pour boiling water into baking pan to surround cups.

Bake about 20 minutes until a knife inserted off-center in custard comes out clean. Remove from baking pan and cool slightly before unmolding. Serve warm or cold. Decorate with toasted coconut.

Makes 4 servings.

GREEN & WHITE JELLIES

3 teaspoons unflavored gelatin powder
3 tablespoons water
5 to 6 tablespoons sugar
Scant 1 cup coconut milk
1/3 cup coconut cream, see page 11
1-1/4 cups water
2 pieces pandanus leaf, each 3 inches long or 3/4 to 1
    teaspoon kewra water
Green food coloring

Sprinkle 1-1/2 teaspoons of the gelatin over 1-1/2 tablespoons water in a small bowl. Let soften 5 minutes, then place bowl over a small saucepan of hot water. Stir until gelatin has dissolved, then remove from heat.

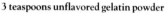

Put 3 tablespoons of the sugar and coconut milk into a medium-size saucepan. Cook, stirring, until sugar has dissolved. Remove from heat and stir in coconut cream.

Stir a little coconut mixture into dissolved gelatin, then return mixture to saucepan and stir. Divide among 4 or 6 individual molds. Place in refrigerator to set.

Put the remaining 2 to 3 tablespoons of sugar (depending on taste), the 1-1/4 cups water and pandanus leaf or kewra water in a medium-size saucepan over low heat. Cook, stirring, until sugar dissolves. Increase heat and bring to a boil. Boil 2 to 3 minutes, cover and remove from heat. Set aside 15 minutes, then remove pandanus leaf, if used.

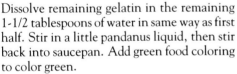

Dissolve remaining gelatin in the remaining 1-1/2 tablespoons of water in same way as first half. Stir in a little pandanus liquid, then stir back into saucepan. Add green food coloring to color green.

Set aside until cold but not set, then pour over set coconut mixture. Place in refrigerator to set. Dip molds into hot water 1 to 2 seconds then turn out onto cold plates.

Makes 4 to 6 servings.

Note: If pandanus leaf or kewra water are unavailable, flavor with rosewater and color pink with red food coloring, to make Pink & White Jellies.

LYCHEES IN COCONUT CUSTARD

3 egg yolks
3 to 4 tablespoons sugar
Scant 1 cup coconut milk
1/3 cup coconut cream, see page 11
About 1 tablespoon triple-distilled rose water
Red food coloring
About 16 fresh lychees, peeled, halved and seeds
  removed
Rose petals to decorate

In a bowl, beat together egg yolks and sugar
until light.

In a medium-size nonstick saucepan, heat
coconut milk to just below boiling, then
slowly stir into sugar mixture. Return to pan
and cook over low heat, stirring with a
wooden spoon, until custard coats the back of
the spoon.

Remove from heat and stir in coconut cream,
rose water to taste and enough red food coloring to color pale pink. Refrigerate until cold,
stirring occasionally. Spoon a thin layer of
custard into 4 small bowls. Arrange lychees
on custard. Decorate with rose petals. Serve
remaining custard separately to pour over
lychees.

Makes 4 servings.

GOLDEN THREADS

6 egg yolks
1 teaspoon egg white
2 cups sugar
Few drops of jasmine extract
1 cup water

Strain egg yolks through cheesecloth into a small bowl. Beat lightly with egg white. In a saucepan, gently heat sugar, jasmine extract and water, stirring until sugar dissolves, then boil until thickened slightly. Adjust heat so syrup is hot but not moving.

Spoon a small amount of egg yolk mixture into a pastry bag fitted with a tip with a very small hole or a cone of waxed paper with a very small hole in the pointed end. Using a circular movement, carefully dribble a trail of egg into syrup, making swirls about 1-1/2 to 2 inches in diameter with a small hole in center. Make a few at a time, cooking each briefly until set.

Using a skewer inserted in the hole in the center of the spiral, transfer each nest to a plate. Continue making similar nests with the remaining egg yolk mixture. When nests are cool, arrange on a clean plate.

Makes 4 servings.

THAI SWEETMEATS

2 ounces split mung beans, rinsed
1/2 cup shredded coconut
1 egg, separated
1/2 cup palm sugar, crushed
3/4 cup water
Few drops of jasmine extract

Put mung beans into a medium-size sauce-pan, and add enough water to cover by 1-1/2 inches. Bring to a boil, reduce heat and simmer 30 to 45 minutes until tender. Drain through a strainer, then mash thoroughly.

Using your fingers, mix coconut and egg yolk with mung beans to make a firm paste. Divide into pieces about the size of a small walnut and shape into egg-shaped balls using a spoon. Put sugar and water into a small sauce-pan over low heat, and heat, stirring, until sugar has dissolved. Increase heat and bring to a boil. Add jasmine extract to taste and keep hot at just below a simmer.

Using a fork, beat egg white well in a small bowl. Using two forks, dip each ball into egg white, then lower balls into syrup. Cook in syrup 2 to 3 minutes. Using a slotted spoon, transfer to a plate. When all balls have been cooked, spoon over a little syrup. Let stand until cold.

Makes about 16.

LIMEADE

6 limes
1/2 cup sugar
3 cups boiling water
Pinch of salt
Ice cubes
Lime slices to serve

Cut each lime in half and squeeze juice.

Place skins in a heatproof pitcher, then stir in sugar followed by boiling water. Cover and let stand 15 minutes.

Stir in salt. Strain into another pitcher and add lime juice. Let cool, then cover and chill. Serve over ice with lime slices.

Makes about 4-1/2 cups.

INDEX

PRINTED IN BELGIUM BY
proost
INTERNATIONAL BOOK PRODUCTION